Tricks
to Pick Up
Chicks

Magic Tricks, Lines, Bets, Scams & Psychology

Rich Ferguson, aka "The Ice Breaker"

You acknowledge that Rich Ferguson or his partners are not liable for any misuse, harm, accidents or embarrassments from attempting any of the scams, tricks, stunts, pranks, bets, lines or tips in this book. This book is intended for entertainment purposes and you play at your own risk of rejection, humiliation, danger or injury. However, if you find that you are the hit of the party, score with women, make lots of new friends, become the coolest guy around, make more money at your job or enjoy life to its fullest, then we take full credit and will accept cash or credit for donation!

Model Photography: *Ely Roberts,* Back Photo: *Mike Larson*
Body Language Model: *Abby Zerger*
Playing Card Art: *Emery Miller,* Cover Illustration: *Chih Hang*
Location/Support: Native Lounge, Big Images, iii Design,
Garret Matsuura, Katin Imes, Christine Dahlquist, Ken Pettit,
Ben Lawless, Laurel Walsh and Traci Ferguson for being Mrs. Right

THEICEBREAKER.COM

Written and Designed by Rich Ferguson, AKA "The Ice Breaker"
www.TheIceBreaker.com

ISBN-10: 1450560180   EAN-13: 9781450560184

"The right man is the one who seizes the moment."

-Johann Wolfgang von Goethe
17th century philosopher of Romanticism

INTRODUCTION

Going into a situation with the confidence to wing it is great if you have all the skills to back it up. However, most people need a game plan if they want to succeed. I've seen Rich at numerous parties and he has no problem approaching the toughest and most skeptical fighters or the most beautiful women. He's not the tallest or the richest guy at the party, but he's got a ton of secret weapons that freak people out. Now *you* have a collection of ice-breakers and tricks to help you become the life of the party.

To be a champion at dating, you have to get out and play the game. Don't know how to approach someone new? Use tricks to get the advantage you're looking for and to have confident fun with ladies wherever you go. In a way, guys out there are losing the fight because they are beating themselves. Get out of your own head and get into theirs! I've seen numerous tricks in action from the man himself. They work. Period. The battle has just begun but you're already ahead of the other guys...

Chuck "The Iceman" Liddell, Champion Fighter

FORWARD

"With great powers come great responsibilities." Strangely, when I heard those words from Peter Parker in Spiderman, I thought of the insane amount of scams and tricks I'm capable of and how lucky the world is that I use them for good. I grew up having to stay a step ahead of people for survival. As a business owner, I've had to keep that skill of adapting alive. As a full time magician, I've mastered what tricks breaks the ice and how to read a person like a book. These skills become apparent to others at my shows. When I'm done performing at a private party, it is amazing how many teenagers and grown men approach me and ask the question, "Can you just show me one simple trick I can do to impress a girl?" This constant request, combined my with vast experience of observation, brought me to create Tricks To Pick Up Chicks. My hope is that men around the world will take a new approach to meeting women. It is not about the tricks, but an excuse and ease to be yourself anytime, anywhere. The tricks in this book hook a lady's interest and let you be yourself in a fun and confident manner- the two things woman want most! Woman aside, the tricks, bets and scams you are about to learn are great fun for life. As a recently married man, I still use these tricks to make my wife smile daily. I have created a collection of nearly self-working miracles perfect for men of any age, personality, confidence level and ability. You are all set. Go out and share all the magic life has to offer... and meet lots of women while you are at it!

THE GOODS!

Chapter 1 - "Quickies"

Quick Tricks, Ice Breakers & Lines

Quick Tricks & Icebreakers

These require little to no permission or interaction. Quickies are tricks you apparently spontaneously spring on someone to break the ice. Enjoy your "Quickies!"

Suck

If you are in a situation with straws and drinks, prepare a straw with a small knot at one end. When a girl looks away, switch her straw for the one with a knot. The reason you switch them rather than try to tie hers is to save a lot of time and minimize the risk of being seen with her drink for more than a split second. The best switch is made by having the tied straw held by your finger tips and thumb with the straw running down the length of your forearm. As you reach past the glass, drop your straw in as you pull her straw out. The arm holding the straw blocks her view. Now sit back and laugh when she eventually tries to drink from her straw!

Tip: Be careful looking suspicious at a bar setting with a stranger's drink. I would only recommend this in mixed company or if you have gotten very quick as switching straws.

All Cracked Up

If you think the fastest way to a girl's heart is to startle her, then you'll love this bone cracking stunt. Get a hard plastic cup and place it under you armpit. Approach a girl or wait for someone to notice that you are moving your head in your hands as if to crack it. In an action as if you are cracking your neck or wrist, coordinate the movement as you crush the hidden cup with your arm. This is the quickest and easiest way to make people jump then laugh.

Tip: Be sure that you use the type of plastic cup that cracks when you smash it and does not simple buckle. They are often clear, stiff plastic.

Let me Get That

This is a little bit more of a scam, but depending on your personality and the setting, this might work wonders. Stand a few feet away from a girl and look at her hair a bit funny. Secretly have a very small piece of some sort of food hidden between your first finger and thumb. Get caught looking a little puzzled and say, "Excuse me, you have something in your hair." She will certainly be a little self conscious and worry where and what it is. Immediately say, "Let me get that." Reach forward and move your fingers into her hair being careful not to use your thumb or first finger. Pull your hands away and drop whatever you had in your fingers. This is a bit underhanded for some, but it establishes contact in an intense sort of way. You've essentially done a basic magic trick but with different reasoning. You could add a bit of sarcasm afterwards and say, "You own me a drink. I don't clean people for nothing."

Linking Pretzels

The next party you are at with pretzels, grab a few pretzels and apparently link them in mid air! Start by secretly breaking half of one of the large loops off a pretzel. Try to make the break as clean as possible so you do not loose any parts of the pretzel. Take a second pretzel and hold it in place hooked on the broken pretzel as you magically fix it back into place. To get the broken loop to stay back in place and link the second pretzel, simply moisten the tips of the broken piece with your

tongue. Force the broken parts in place for 30 seconds and they will be bonded as good as new. Now you have a linked pretzel. At this point, hold the linked pretzels by only showing part of one sticking out at your finger tips. The other linked pretzel is hidden in your hand. In the other hand, display a third (a second pretzel as far as the viewer is aware of) individual pretzel. You are going to act as if you link the two shown pretzels together as you come down and keep the individual pretzel in your hand.

Tip: To create the illusion that the pretzels link in mid air, you can bring the tips of the pretzels together and apparently toss them both into the air. Of course, you only toss only the linked set into the air as you keep the other one in your hand. You can slightly pull back the individual pretzel so it is not seen and be sure to keep your hand natural so it does not look like you are hiding something. If you really want a challenge and make this look perfect, try to throw the linked pretzel into the other hand as you toss and catch the individual pretzel into the hand the linked one came from! The goal is to make it look like you just tossed one pretzel onto another and they appear linked immediately. As an easy version, you can simply place the individual pretzel into the hand holding the linked one and give that hand a slight shake or gesture. Perhaps, even have her blow on it! Then remove the linked pretzels while pinching and hiding the other single pretzel.

Tongue Tied

The next time you are at a party with cherries in sight, snag a stem off a cherry and tie a knot in it. Hide this in your mouth between your bottom teeth and your cheek or lip. Walk directly up to a girl that has a cherry, desert with a cherry or a drink with a cherry and instantly say, "Oh! Can I have that stem..." Without hesitation, just take it and place it in your mouth. With your tongue, place it on the opposite side of your mouth and get the pre-tied one to your lips within a few seconds! Pull it out and leave it on a napkin like it is no big deal. Walk away and come back later unless you immediately have her with her jaw on the floor.

Right Number

Far too often, phones are laying around in plain sight. If you can easily get away with it, grab a girls phone and call yourself. Once you have her number and she is back with her phone, call her and say hi. Better yet, try to string her along like you are a telemarketer as you walk toward her and let her discover you are messing with her.

What do you Think?

In a mall or store ask your dream-girl's opinion on an item. Perhaps you can legitimately ask about a gift you are buying your sister to get her talking about something they know about. Be sure to compliment her on something she is wearing or buying. Ask for her number so you can follow up and tell her how it worked out. If you got her number, give her the gift on your first date!

Something in my Eye?

If sitting in sight of someone you want to tease and freak out, try this eye bursting prank out. Grab one of those personal creamers out of bowl and hide it in your hand. Have it where the lid that pulls back is facing down in your fist. Hold the creamer in place with your thumb and bottom few fingers as you apparently use your first finger tip to pull at your eye like you have something in it. Blink a few times and turn to a girl and say, "Dang it. It seems as if something is poking my eye." Rub your eye again. Grab your fork and bring it up carefully as if you are going to use it to dig around your eye with it. You might carefully pull a little on the bottom eyelid to make her nervous. At this point, you have her attention. Cover your eye with the hand and fingers that are hiding the creamer and stick

the fork into the lid to break the seal. From behind your hand, white cream should shoot out of what appears to be your eye!

Stuck Up

If sitting at a table or bar that has salt and pepper shakers, make one float for no apparent reason. To prepare for the trick, break off about half of a toothpick and hide it between your thumb and middle finger so it runs along the inside of your finger. The tip of the toothpick is about flush to the tips of your finger tips and sticks out just enough so that you can jam the

point into a hole in the shaker top. To do the trick, reach toward the shaker, push the finger tips onto the top and lift. Do the same motion with the free hand and when you are about to place the shaker back down, the free hand moves first to grab the shaker and hand it over. As a side note, knowing these simple tricks are great for those times when someone might ask you to pass the salt. You might have to be prepared, but these tricks go a long way in breaking the ice.

Note Test

Write down on a piece of paper, "Smile if you want sex." Fold it in half and slide it in front of a someone. The funny thing is that it is very difficult to not smile or laugh at this silly and outrageous note! Score 1-0. After this ice-breaker, it should be easy enough to laugh about it.

Floating Roll

Your mom always told you to stop playing with your food! Well, you are grown up and now and it's okay. To make a dinner roll look like it is floating, you will need a fork, a dinner roll and a napkin. Put the fork on the back of a napkin with the handle of the fork held pinched with your first two finger tips and thumb. Your other hand holds the opposite corner in the exact same way but without a fork being secretly held. The fork is on your side of the napkin angled toward the center of the napkin when held up like a curtain. You do not let the spectator know you have a fork being held. To do the illusion, lower the napkin onto a dinner roll and lightly stab the roll with the

fork. Slowly bring the napkin up while stretched across the fingers and show the dinner roll is now missing. At this point, arch your thumbs upwards a bit to push the roll into the napkin center. From the spectators view, they will see a floating dinner roll hovering into the napkin. You can easily rotate the corners of the napkin and manipulate the fork to make the roll come to the top edge of the napkin as if it floated to the top and rests balanced on the napkin's edge. In addition, when the roll is pushed into the dead center of the napkin, you can move the entire unit around with your arms keeping the roll in the center. This will give the illusion that the roll is floating all over the place and that you are keeping up with it.

Nose Plug

Pulling something out of your nose might not be the right "move" for everyone but everyone is different and every situation is different. This effect looks like you pull a long piece of paper out of your nose. To set this up, remove a straw from its wrapper and fold the paper back and forth on itself like an accordion. When you stick this folded gimmick into your nose, you can pull on one end to make it all unfold and look as if you pulled a foot long piece of paper out of your nose. I'd only recommend this type of stunt to freak out a girl or tease them in school.

Up Yours

To make it look like you shoved an entire straw or pencil up your nose is easy. Hold a straw by the finger tips of your first two or three fingers and your thumb. Place the end of the straw at the base of your nose on an angle that looks like you can put it part way up your nose. However, stick the end slightly towards the center of the nose so the skin will keep it from traveling up. Your arm and hand are angled in line with your nose and the straw. Push slightly upwards and let the straw slide between your finger tips and hide it behind your arm or down your sleeve. Give an upward jerk of your head and a nice sniff to amplify the look. At this point, the tip of the straw is just at your finger tips and it is an easy matter to move your finger tips toward your mouth and grab the tip of the straw with your teeth and pull the straw "from your mouth". This illusion is simple and bizarre once you have the timing down.

Impossible Straw

To make a straw apparently appear from your mouth or finger tips, you'll need to modify it. Take a straw and carefully cut it along one entire edge from end to end. Be sure this is not a cut that twists around the straw. Once you have a straight cut, you can open one end up flat and roll the straw onto itself. You roll from one end all the way to the other until you have a little roll. This roll, as you'll quickly discover, will pop into a full straw if you let it go! It's quite amazing how fun this is. You can load this gimmicked straw in any area it can fit and by pulling on just the tail end piece, you can pull out what looks like a straw from nowhere. Have a duplicate straw near you or in your lap to switch casually before handing it to someone.

Blow on it

The next time you are sitting at a table with a straw and a dream-girl, try this simple trick out. Mention that straws have energy or static like balloons. If you rub them, they will be attracted to you. Rub one on her and place it between the two of you. Be sure the straw is perpendicular to you. As you gesture with your hands and as you have her gesture with her hands to summon the straw, lightly blow on it! It will roll towards her. You can also leave her out of this and just do this randomly as if you are using energy to push the straw away from you.

Mistaken Vanish

Your dream-girl watches as you apparently make a small object in your hand vanish. You use a straw or pencil as a magic wand to wave over the object. After a couple waves, the object stays but the straw vanishes! This is an old classic. If you have not seen this, you need to get out more. Lay an object (like a coin) in one palm and hold a straw or pencil in the other hand. You are going to stick the straw behind your ear to vanish it so be sure that ear is away from the person watching. Hold out your hand with the object and motion with the straw. Bring it up towards the ear once, then twice while staring directly at the object. Say, "It's gonna vanish!" and on the third lifting of the straw, leave it behind your ear and come down just like before. Instantly close the hand around the object and say, "It's gone!" Often, they will demand that you open your hand. Do so with a smirk and gesture that it was the straw that vanished, not the object. As they grab at the object, you might have plenty of opportunity to remove the straw and make it "appear" behind their ear. If you can time it, simply remove the straw and reach toward them and pull it along the top of their ear, letting the straws entire length drag on their ear. Hold the straw at the very tip to give the illusion the straw came from far away behind their head.

Knife Swallowing

Want some iron in your diet? Try this one out to make her do a double take. This quick trick comes down to simple angles and some simple acting. Place a knife near the edge of a table in front of you. While sitting keep your knees together below the edge of the table. Grab the knife with both hands with the thumbs holding the one flat side of the knife and the fingers

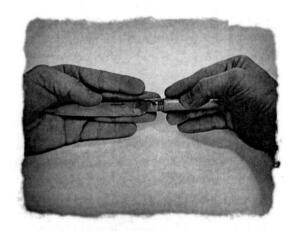

pointing towards each other holding the other flat side. Lift your hands off the table concealing the knife. Keeping your hands and arms flat from elbow to elbow, rotate one arm to expose the end of the knife as you gesture toward your mouth to swallow it. Pause for a second here to make sure you have a good breath. At the same time, bring the arms and hands down just to the table's edge and let the knife drop onto your lap. It is very important that you do not open your hands or move your thumbs. This dropping action is secret. All in one action, come back up for the real swallow except this time there is nothing in your hands. From the spectators view, it should look like you brought a knife to your mouth, pulled away for a second to get a breath and then proceeded to lower a knife into your mouth. At the point at which you are supposedly lowering a knife into your mouth, finish with the hands coming apart at the point the knife would be in the mouth completely. Pretend to be pushing the last bit of the "knife" into your throat. Remember, you are actually holding nothing and you just need it to look like you're struggling to get the last little bit of knife in the mouth. Pull your hands away and give one last difficult swallow and head tilt to finish it off.

Cigarette Vanish

If you are in a setting where someone is smoking, you can try this cigarette vanish. You are going to hold your fingers in a strange position to make this work. Hold your hands out in front of you flat down. Bend your thumbs into your palms. Curl your first finger of each hand down to meet the area just below the finger nail and above the first knuckle of the thumb. This is the position you are going to hold the cigarette to vanish it. The secret here is that the cigarette will stick to one of your thumb nails by wetting it. Just before you grab a cigarette, lick or moisten the back of one of your thumb nails. Hold the cigarette in the position explained. After a few moments, the paper in the cigarette will stick fairly well to your nail. Lift the cigarette in the strange holding position up by both ends to show it to someone. To vanish it, quickly open all your fingers as if you flicked the cigarette into nowhere. What is really going on is the cigarette is hidden behind the opened thumb! Reverse the movements to get it to return.

Doll Head

For a very quick laugh and test for personality, approach someone with a coin and say "Heads or tails?" No matter what they say, you reveal a little head from a tiny doll and say, "Heads!" To make the head appear, hold it in the opposite hand of the coin. Toss the coin up and catch it in the hand that held it. When you bring the hand down to catch the coin, throw the other hand onto it to secure the coin. What you are really doing is putting the doll head right onto the coin. You can also improve this handling by catching the coin and rotating this hand downward onto the hand with the doll head and not letting the coin drop to the hand that holds that doll head. If you choose the second version, start with the hand that holds the doll head face down and the one with the coin face up. After catching the coin rotate the hands opposite directions onto each other for the illusion. It is mostly a gag and laugh, so do not worry about your sleight of hand being precise.

It's Going to Blow

If outside, hiking or at a park, take a swig of a drink and keep it hidden in your mouth. Gesture towards your nose as if you need to clear it. To freak someone out, hold your hand to the side of your nose and mouth to hide the fact that you blow the liquid from your mouth. Be sure to block the side of the nose toward the person that is looking. Move your head as if the liquid came from your nose. Right afterwards, wipe your nose.

Killer Bee

A great way to make someone freak out then laugh with you is to fake a bee attack. This is great in parks or crossing the street. While walking near a girl you want to make laugh, start dipping and weaving out of the way of a bee. Wave your hands, run back and forth and then run towards her! Don't worry about a bee not being there because nobody would see it anyways.

Gotta Go

If walking on the streets, in parks, alleyways or outside, pretend to be peeing to shock someone. If you have access to one of those devices used to remove mucus from a kids nose, squeeze it and fill it with water. It is easy to hide this in your hand and pretend to be peeing at any given notice. Of course, block the view so nobody can tell what is going on. If a girl is screaming at you, you can even turn towards her and get her wet with the water. I shouldn't have to say this, but "shock" tricks like these can break the ice, but be sure you are only doing it if the situation seems right for you.

Wanna Kiss?

Get a couple different types of Hershey's Kisses. Hold one in each hand and approach your dream-girl. Tell her that she is so beautiful that you just have to share a kiss with her. Pause for a second and then show both hands, "Do you want milk chocolate or almonds?" If she was very receptive to your first offer, you might want to give her the chocolate after the kiss!

High Five

One of the quickest ways to test if someone is worth your time, personality wise, is the high five test. Have a group of friends near a girl you are eyeing. Walk right toward your friends giving high fives to people, including your dream-girl. You might give her a little extra by holding on to her hand with a little more curl in your fingers and continue on to your friends. If she seemed receptive, go back and do some tricks. If she was irritated by the gesture, no harm because you certainly didn't do this for her in anyone's eyes... even though you did. You'd be amazed at how this easy test takes people off guard and puts them in a instant mood to want to talk to you and hang out.

Bar Mouse

The next time you have access to a paper napkin and lemon, try this out. Twist each corner of the napkin like a handmade cigarette. Twist the corners so they are all facing downwards

and there is a ballooning effect in the middle. Place this curved napkin with strange points on each corner onto a lemon. It should just hover above the surface. Give it a push down the bar or over the table and yell, "Bar mouse!" It will roll and wobble like something is really crawling! The girl you are trying to make jump may hate you after this but there's just a fine line between love and hate. You are closer than you were before!

It's Nothing

If the situation arrises that a girl drops a coin or something small at a bar, simply reach down to "pick it up" with the toes of your shoe about 6 inches or less from the coin. As you look like you grab the coin or object with you fingers, you simply flick it under your shoe as you close your fingers toward your thumb. Then you apparently bring up the coin or object. It vanishes from your fingers as you drop nothing into her hand. Give a little wink or smile as you walk away.

Pick Up Lines

Keep in mind that memorizing lines does not do anything if you are not interesting. You are simply trying to break the ice and show personality. Just keep this frame of mind when using your tricks and lines. Too often, guys use lines and think they are magic words to hypnotize women. Women hear them all the time and it is your approach and reasoning that is key. You want to be clever, confident, fun, charming and genuine. You need to be able to laugh at how bad lines are as well. As stated before, you are breaking the ice and using a line as a tool to instantly show confidence and personality. It's more of the delivery than the line itself.

"Well, here I am, what are your other two wishes?"

"Maybe we can go out sometime and get a bowl of cereal."

Pick up a pack of sugar that actually says, "sugar" on it then say, "You dropped your name tag!" Immediately laugh with her and do a trick with it.

If you see a woman with a Guess shirt on take a guess at her breast size and say something like, "Hmm, I'm guessing 32-C?"

"I'm going outside to make out... care to join me?"

"I came over here because I noticed you were staring at my butt."- when she wasn't.

"What does a guy with a 13 inch penis have for breakfast?" ... "Well, I had eggs, toast, juice..."

Chapter 1 - "Quickies"

"I'm thinking of a number between 1 and 10. What is it?" ... Regardless of what she says, say, "Wrong! Take off your clothes."

"I'm going outside to talk to my next girlfriend. Care to join me?"

"Give me three good reasons why I shouldn't buy you a drink."

"I'm known for making amazing predictions... You are not wearing underwear... Oh, you are? Oh, I guess I was just predicting the future!"

"Do you know the essential difference between sex and conversation? No? Want to go upstairs and talk?"

"I bet you $20 you're gonna turn me down."

"I've had quite a bit to drink, and you're beginning to look pretty good."

"If I told you that you had a great body, would you hold it against me?"

"My boys over there bet that I wouldn't be able to start a conversation with the most beautiful girl in the room. Want to buy some drinks with their money?"

"Do you believe in love at first sight or should I walk by you again?"

"Sex (or fill in the blank) is not the answer. Sex (or fill in the blank) is the question. "Yes" is the answer."

"If God is watching us, the least we can do is be entertaining. Want to see a magic trick?"

"I intend to find my dream girl tonight. So far, so good."

"Does this rag smell like chloroform to you?"

"I have never understood why women love cats. Cats are independent, they don't listen, they don't come in when you call, they like to stay out all night, and when they're home they like to be left alone and sleep. In other words, every quality that women hate in a man, they love in a cat."

"Girls are like roads, the more curves, the more dangerous they are."

"I don't have a beer gut, I have a protective covering for my rock hard abs."

"Panties aren't the best thing on earth, but next to it."

"Without nipples, breasts would be pointless."

"According to a new survey, women say they feel more comfortable undressing in front of men than they do undressing in front of other women. They say that women are too judgmental, where, of course, men are just grateful."

"What if there were no hypothetical questions?"

"I'm a humble person, really. I'm actually much greater than I think I am."

"Why is a bra singular and panties plural?"

"Without ME, it's just AWESO."

"I always take life with a grain of salt, ...plus a slice of lemon, ...and a shot of tequila. What do you want to drink?"

"Sex on TV can't hurt ...unless you fall off."

"Hey, have you seen God's gift to women? Well, look no further!"

"If it were any more crowded in here, you'd be on my lap."

Chapter 1 - "Quickies"

"Is this seat taken?" ... "No? Good. Because if it was, you'd be having drinks with the Invisible Man."

When ordering and waiting for food, tell a girl, "I wish I ate half as good as you do." If she replies that she does alway eat healthy or admits that she sometimes eats bad, ask her if you could get together and get some tips on a healthy lifestyle. Ask for her number. When she gives you her number act surprised that it was not a business card for a dietician.

"Your feet must be tired. You've been running through my mind all night."

"I've had this fantasy of you in my head all night... I just don't know if you can live up to it."

"Oh, wow! You look like my future girlfriend!"

One Liners

"Women might be able to fake orgasms. But men can fake a whole relationship."

"Men have two emotions: Hungry and Horny. If you see him without an erection, make him a sandwich."

"Having sex is like playing bridge. If you don't have a good partner, you'd better have a good hand."

"Evening news is where they begin with 'Good evening', and then proceed to tell you why it isn't."

"I saw a woman wearing a sweat shirt with "Guess" on it...so I said "Implants?""

"Women will never be equal to men until they can walk down the street with a bald head and a beer gut, and still think they are sexy."

"I didn't say it was your fault, I said I was blaming you."

"Good girls are bad girls that never get caught."

"Behind every successful man is his woman. Behind the fall of a successful man is usually another woman."

"There's a fine line between cuddling and holding someone down so they can't get away."

"A little boy asked his father, "Daddy, how much does it cost to get married?" Father replied, "I don't know son, I'm still paying.""

"Why is it that most nudists are people you don't want to see naked?

Chapter 1 - "Quickies"

"Virginity is like a soap-bubble, one prick and it is gone."

"Good health is merely the slowest possible rate at which one can die."

"The big difference between sex for money and sex for free is that sex for money usually costs a lot less."

"Life's a bitch, 'cause if it were a slut, it'd be easy."

"If you can stay calm while all around you is chaos, then you probably haven't completely understood the situation."

"Women should not have children after 35. 'Really...' 35 children are enough."

"It matters not whether you win or lose: what matters is whether I win or lose."

"Don't piss me off! I'm running out of places to hide the bodies."

"Clinton lied. A man might forget where he parks or where he lives, but he never forgets oral sex, no matter how bad it is."

"Why is it called Alcoholics ANONYMOUS when the first thing you do is stand up and say, 'My name is Peter and I am an alcoholic'?"

"I tried to hang myself with a bungee cord. I kept almost dying."

"Think of how stupid the average person is, and realize half of them are stupider than that."

Lines if She Blows You Off

Guys, there's no need to be a punk. Try to say these with a bit of sarcasm and with gratitude for saving you time. It's her loss and if you handle yourself correctly, she'll realize it.

"I may not be the best looking guy in here, but I'm the only one talking to you."

If she says something to get you to check out, say, "That's what every girl says that's into me. Can't you get an original line?"

"Light travels faster than sound. This's why some people appear bright until you hear them speak."

"Do you like to dance? Well then, could you go dance so I can talk to your friend?"

"God must love stupid people. He made SO many."

"Never get into fights with ugly people, they have nothing to lose."

"Money can't buy happiness, but it sure makes misery easier to live with."

"Some people hear voices. Some see invisible people. Others have no imagination whatsoever."

"Some mistakes are too much fun to only make once." - After you come back again!

"I don't have an attitude problem. You have a perception problem."

"Well aren't you a waste of two billion years of evolution."

Chapter 1 - "Quickies"

"I don't have an attitude; I have a personality you can't handle."

"Millions of sperm and you were the fastest?"

"I guess they call it "PMS" because "mad cow disease" was already taken.

"Only dead fish go with the flow."

"Why don't you slip into something more comfortable...like a coma."

"I'm multi-talented: I can talk and piss you off at the same time."

"You were such an ugly kid. When you played in the sandbox the cat kept covering you up."

"It's so simple to be wise. Just think of something stupid to say and then don't say it."

"I like long walks, especially when they are taken by people who annoy me." -Then don't leave.

"I never test the depth of the water with both feet. Thanks for saving me trouble."

"Your gene pool could use a little chlorine."

"Everyone has the right to be stupid, but you are abusing the privilege!"

"It was love at first sight. Then I took a second look!"

"Take it easy... It ain't the jeans that make your butt look fat."

"If I had a nickel for every time I saw a girl as beautiful as you I'd have about... 5 cents."

"Experience is what you get when you didn't get what you wanted."

"The early bird might get the worm, but the second mouse gets the cheese."

"Some people are like Slinkies … not really good for anything, but you can't help smiling when you see one tumble."

"He doesn't need a parachute to skydive. He only needs a parachute to skydive twice."

"You broke his heart. Let me help you feel better. Check out this trick."

"Ouch, poor guy… It's not the fall that kills you; it's the sudden stop at the end."

"Some cause happiness wherever they go. Others whenever they go."

"There's a fine line between cuddling and holding someone down so they can't get away."

"Women may not hit harder, but they hit lower."

"If at first you don't succeed, skydiving is not for you!"

"See, the problem is that God gives men a brain and a penis, and only enough blood to run one at a time."

"Some of us learn from the mistakes of others; the rest of us have to be the others."

"Constipated people don't give a crap."

Chapter 2 - "One Night Stands"

Magic Tricks, Bar Bets & Scams

Simple Magic Techniques

There are some very basic card forces and sleights to learn. You only have to learn the one you need. All of these are extremely easy and will save your butt when you need to perform and do not know what to do. You may skip ahead and look at the tricks, but just skim over and get the gist of the methods here so you can come back later when needed. For simplicity, I'm going to refer to you often as the magician and the girl or person you are doing the tricks on as the spectator.

Simple Object Vanish

Mission: Knowing a basic sleight of hand move to make a coin or small object vanish will help you with girls, friends and kids the rest of your life. The best technique that does not takes years to master is called the Retention Vanish. Essentially, you hold an object in your hand and it is apparently taken by the other when placed into it face down. You open your hand and it's gone.

Secret: You actually keep it held back with your thumb when turning the hand downward.

How to do it: Here's how to put it all together correctly. Start with an object toward the finger tip of one hand. Hold the object slightly up with your hand to display it and let the object poke out beyond the finger tips. The side of your hand with your finger nails is toward the spectator and your thumb is towards you. Hold your other hand out comfortably in front of you with its palm up and ready to have something placed into it. Begin to place the object from the finger tips onto the open hand. The instant the object is touching the open hand, curl your open hand's fingers up to block the fact that you leave nothing. The hand holding the object can easily pull the object back a little with the thumb from underneath. Remember, this is happening under your hand and behind the curled finger of another. Continue to look as if you left the object under the curled fingers of the awaiting hand and pull the hand out of the side beneath the closing curled fingers. The hand that is actually holding the object still should have its fingers together yet relaxed, however no object is peeking out the tips. Pull the hand that still holds the object casually away but focus all of your attention on the closed empty hand. Done all together, it is a very simple and powerful vanish. To enhance this technique, the starting point of the hand holding the object can be face up. This is to show the side of the hand that has the thumb holding the object. When you go towards the hand that is palm up ready to retrieve the object, the holding hand twists

face down similar to before. The timing paints a solid picture of fairness in the minds of the onlooker. Try this in a mirror and you'll be amazed how easy it is. Lastly, the "move" of pulling the object back with the thumb makes it look like there is no object still showing once you remove your hand from the other. To prove how deceptive this move is, start with the object not even sticking out past the finger tips and simply hold it hidden with the thumb to begin with. However, hold it face up so the object can be seen. Now rotate this hand face down onto the

other and grab nothing as you close those fingers. Pull the hand holding the object away as before. Perhaps, this might be an easier version to start with. Any way you slice it, it will appear that there is an object in a closed hand. When you eventually open it, the object will be gone. Have fun!

Card Control by Overhand Shuffling

Mission: To control the bottom card of the deck (or top card if deck is face up).

Secret: The spectator thinks the cards are being shuffled but there is a section of cards that is never mixed, leaving the bottom card remaining to be forced later.

How to do it: With the cards face down, have the selected card on the bottom. (Note that you could do this face up with the force card being the original top card of the deck... but learn it this bottom-card way first.) Place the cards cradled in the left palm leaning onto the fingers of the left hand. The thumb of the left hand and middle fingers of the left hand will overlap the edges of the cards or press the cards together. Your thumb might not be long enough to grab around the top edge, so it may just rest onto the card backs. This will allow the right thumb and middle fingers to pull out cards from the center of the pack! With the right hand, put the thumb on the short end towards you and the tip of the middle fingers on the

far short edge of the deck. Pull out any amount of cards from the center of the pack upwards and let the rest of the cards fall onto the gap left behind. Take the remaining cards and place them (still gripped by the right thumb and middle finger) on top of the deck. It is easy to pull off the top portion of those cards with your left thumb. Repeat several times to diminish the section you removed. To finish up, you may set down all the cards as you pull one last section from the middle of the pack and place it on top of the deck. This illusion really looks fair. However, the bottom portion of cards that is overlapped by the left middle fingers is never taken. Therefore, the bottom card is always going to remain the bottom card! Most importantly, the finger tips of the left hand are keeping you from taking the bottom section of cards with the right hand. From here, you can force the bottom card when necessary! If this shuffle was done face up, the same action would cause the current top card of the deck to remain unchanged. Try it, too. Bottoms up to you!

Card Force by Criss-Cross Cutting

Mission: To force the top card of the deck, making it the spectator's selected card.

Secret: The spectator thinks they cut to a freely chosen card, but it is simply the top card all along!

How to do it: Place the card you want to force on the top of the deck. Have a spectator cut anywhere they want. Gesture with your hands what to do. Motion and show the cutting action of placing the top half of the deck next to the bottom half. Once they cut the deck halves next to each other, say, "Let's mark where you cut." Place the remaining cards like an "X" on top of the cut cards they just placed down. The card that is to be forced is below the top half you just placed down. At this

point, distract the spectators from focusing too much on the deck by talking about something else for a short moment. Talk about the trick you are about to perform. Talk about the fact that you are going to show all the cards in a moment to prove they are all different. Talk about anything. After that, simply say, "Take a look at the card you cut to and please make sure you remember it!" What you do while saying this is remove the top portion and point to the original top card! This is a complete bluff but cannot be reversed engineered easily since there was no real pressure or suspiciousness to begin with. They really believe their card was chosen fairly! Trust me, this always fools people and you just have to try it to see the beauty in it. It would take years to master some of the insane forces magicians know. If you want to cut to the chase, do this force and move on to talking with your dream-girl.

Card Force by Strip Shuffling

Mission: To force the bottom card of the deck.

Secret: As you are shuffling/stripping cards off the top of the deck, the bottom card always stays on the bottom!

How to do it: Place the card to be forced on the bottom of the deck. Hold the entire pack from above with the right thumb and middle finger along the sides of the deck and toward one end of the pack, allowing the entire pack to stick out toward your left hand. This will allow the left hand to grab from underneath

and remove packets of cards off the top of the deck. The tricky part is that you are going to pull chunks of cards onto your left hand with your left hand. These cards will all come from the top of the deck being held by the right finger tips. Pull off chunks of cards off the top of the pack onto your left hand. After you have pulled a packet of cards off the top of the deck, let that packet drop into the left palm. Repeat the action. When pulling the next chunk of cards away onto the left hand, be sure to make close contact with the remaining deck and packets that have been already removed. This will look like you are removing chunks of cards from the middle of the deck. In ac-

tuality, it is a very fair shuffle/stripping motion. The only thing people do not notice is that the bottom card of the right pack is always the bottom of the original pack! This is your card you are forcing! As you are pulling these little chunks off into the left hand, instruct your spectator to tell you to stop. Once the spectator tells you to stop, simply lift up the right hand packet and show them the bottom card. Have them remember it (or remove it if the trick calls for it) and continue with the trick. You have just forced a card that seems 100% free choice without learning years of sleight of hand!

One Way Deck Set Up

Some card tricks will call for the One Way method of locating a card. This is quite simple!

Mission: A card is picked and placed back into the deck. The cards can be shuffled but you always can locate the card.

Secret: Many decks in stores have unique designs on them. If you were to take a cheap deck, you'll see that the designs are all the same direction. Removing one card and reversing it end for end will make the design upside down and easy to locate! However, this might be a little too obvious depending on the design. You might find a design that has a subtle difference or mark one end of regular deck with a pen. I often take a regular deck that has no difference end to end and fill in a random dot in a design toward the upper left corner of one end of the cards with a marker than matches the back color. Either way you decide to do this, the trick here is that you can see if a card is reversed when flipping through or spreading the cards.

How to do it: To do this, have a person choose any card they want from your prepared deck and have them remember it. The instant they take their card out, turn the deck half way and square it up on the table. Continue to rotate the deck completely around the rest of the way when you pick the cards back up. You may choose to just rotate the deck end for end in your lap instead. You know what to do whichever way you choose. Once the deck is rotated end for end, have her stick her card in anywhere she wants. You may shuffle the cards now as long as you remember to keep the cards all facing the same direction. To find the card is a cinch as you look at the backs. You will determine the best way to look at the backs depending on the trick. You can easily spread the cards across the table and secretly look for the reversed card or look at the backs of the cards as you deal cards one at a time. It will be the only reversed card. This set up will help you in several tricks you will learn later.

Card Tricks

These are tricks that you can do with little to no setup and practice. You do not have to be a master magician to be clever. However, the more skill you actually have, the better! You can demonstrate most of these tricks to impress girls or make new friends. You're about to learn some basic techniques, cards tricks, tricks with money, mind reading tricks and tricks with everyday objects. Good luck with your "One Night Stands."

Wet Napkin

Effect: A card is picked and lost into the deck. A napkin on the counter has liquid poured on it and the card magically appears.

Secret: A duplicate card that matches the one you force is under a napkin. When a napkin gets wet, it automatically makes the card appear.

Performance: Force a card by one of the two methods described in Magic Techniques. Whichever card you forced, have a duplicate of that card hidden face up under the top napkin at the table. You are set to go. After she remembers the card she "picked", have her shuffle the cards. Take the cards back and hold up random cards asking if they are correct. She will think your trick sucks. After a couple attempts and a little effort on your part, take your drink and pour some onto the napkins that have been in plain sight the whole time. This will saturate the napkin and make it see through. The card will magically start to appear through the paper! While this is happening, you might consider taking the cards and putting them away so she doesn't go through them! Here's how to take this to take this to another level. When you are looking through the cards to show her some during the trick, you might put the selection on top or bottom so it will be easy to remove it later. This is so you can leave it in your pocket when she wants to check the cards.

Happy Birthday

Effect: You notice it is someone's birthday. This is really common at parties, clubs, bars and restaurants. Any card is picked from a girl. You cut open the deck and have the card replaced. You then spell out "Happy Birthday" plus her name. The very next card is her card!

Secret: You need to do two things. One, learn what the person's name is before walking up. Two, when she takes the card, quickly turn away and count 13 cards plus how many letters for her name. Hold this section a little separate onto of the rest of the cards. When you turn back around, pull off this "random" chunk of cards and have her cards replaced into the deck. You are all set to do the trick.

Performance: Start by letting them shuffle the cards. Any card can be picked. Take the rest of the cards and turn around so that you cannot see the chosen card being shown to friends. What you really are doing is counting 13 cards for "Happy Birthday" plus her name. Keep these cards a little separate with your finger above the rest of the cards. Turn around and open up the pack and gesture to put the card back. Place the rest of the cards on top. If you can do the *Overhand Shuffle* and not mess up the top half of the deck, go for it. Otherwise, you can just continue easily from here. Ask what the girls name is even though you already overheard it earlier while checking her out and watching her friends. Proceed to spell out something like, "H-A-P-P-Y-B-I-R-T-H-D-A-Y-M-A-R-Y". Let her turn over the next card! It will be her card. This simple trick will really put on smile on her face because it was custom for her and nobody knew that you already knew her name.

69

Effect: Two cards are picked and lost back into the pack randomly. The cards are picked up by you and tossed into the other hand. However, the two chosen cards stay behind!

Secret: You set up the deck with four cards on top and execute the *Criss-Cross Cut Force*. Place the cards in this order. Six of Clubs, Nine of Spades, Six of Spades followed by Nine of Clubs on top all face down onto the deck. The real trick here is that people won't remember the difference between the two cards they picked and the two that you end up showing them.

Performance: Let them cut the cards according to the *Criss-Cross Cut*. Instruct them to take the top two cards they "cut to." They take their Nine of Clubs and Six of Spades. Place the rest of those cards onto the other half of the deck. Remember, you have two more cards on top that you are using in this trick! As they are looking at their cards, simply slide your top card onto the bottom of the deck. So now you have a Six of Clubs on top of your deck and a Nine of Spades on the bottom! Have her place her cards back into the pack anywhere she wants. This is the killer part! Keeping the deck face down as not to reveal a similar looking card to hers and grab the top and bottom of the cards with your finger tips and thumb of one hand. Your finger tips are along the middle of the bottom facedown card and your thumb is on the top center of the back of the top card. You are going to toss the entire deck into the other hand except you will keep the top and bottom cards! This is almost self working. Just try it! Simply pull back and toss all the cards onto the other hand. By slightly pressing, the finger tips and thumb retain the top and bottom card! It's self working magic at it's best! Show the two cards and watch her jaw will drop. Although they are the opposite, it's extremely difficult to remember because of the fact that 6 and 9 can be upside down from each other and look the same and those two suits mixed with those numbers is confusing. I guarantee you will love doing this simple self working effect.

Magic in Her Pocket

Effect: A girl shuffles the pack and they are placed into her pocket. She fairly picks a card through process of free choices out loud. She then gets to decide how many cards down from the top of the deck is that card! You reach into her pocket (nice bonus) and remove cards one at a time until you reach the chosen number. Sure enough, it is the card!

Secret: When the cards are shuffled and placed into the pocket (your pocket if she does not have one), it is very easy to see what the bottom card is! This is the card that is forced in a special way. The card is forced by giving choices that are not choices after all. When she eventually is led to that card choice, she gets to decide how many cards down from the top of the deck is her card. You simply pull cards off the top of the deck when reaching into the pocket. When you get to the right number, just remove the bottom card!

Performance: The real key here is the performance of the choices to force that bottom card you looked at before putting the cards away. Let's just say, for sake of argument, that the bottom card was a 5 of Spades. I would say, "There are four suits in a deck. Hearts, Clubs, Diamonds and Spades. We are going to get rid of a couple, name two." The key to the wording is that you never specifically say that you are keeping or getting rid of what they say so you can go with whatever you need to happen! If they name two which include that one you need to force, then continue to have them pick one of those. If they picked the two that do not include your force, say, "I said we are going to get rid of a couple suits. Do you have something against... Well, regardless, we have Spades and ... left. We need to get rid of one of those. Pick one." Make her end up with what you need. Continue this type of back and forth "choice" with her for the card value as well. For instance, "You chose Spades. Of all the spades, there are high cards and low cards. We need to eliminate one of them. Pick one." If she picks low, then I'd say, "Oh, low cards. Great. That would be something like 2, 3, 4, and 5 of Spades. We need to get rid of some of those as well. Pick two." Do you see the rhythm here?

Whatever you need to make happen, just do it. The phrasing leaves it open ended on what is going to happen so you can adjust accordingly. Be careful not to be obvious and say things like, "You picked Spades and Hearts. We will get rid of Clubs and Diamonds then." Do not make the mistake of trying to explain what you are doing or make a big mention of the cards you are removing unless it worked out in your favor perfectly. From here, it is a simple matter to continue the trick as mentioned before. She has been forced the bottom card and now she can be asked, "You picked the 5 of Spades. You shuffled the cards. I have not touched them. The 5 of Spades is in the deck somewhere. How many cards down from the top of the deck do you think it is?" Here's the fun part. You get to reach inside her pocket and remove cards one at a time! At the number she picked, remove the bottom card instead and you have a miracle.

Fastest Card Trick

Effect: She shuffles the cards and you take the deck. You hold up any card toward her and you tell her what it is.

Secret: You are able to see the card face even while it's back is toward you!

Performance: There a couple easy ways to get a glimpse of the card you are holding without any practice at all. One, passing the card over dark coffee, silverware or reflective surface. When taking the card, pass it over the reflective surface and do not stare at the reflection.

Just a quick glance is all you need. From her angle, she will not see the card in the reflection, so your secret is safe. However, for a hands-on version, learn the following! When you take a card, hold the short ends between your thumb (bottom)

and finger tips (top). Hold the card directly toward the girl. If you bend the card ends toward her, you will be able to peek into the bend and see the card value in the left bottom corner! It is amazing at how little you have to bend it and how impossible it seems from the girl's perspective that you can see the card.

Which Row?

I'm not a big fan of obvious math card tricks unless they are disguised a bit. Here's a great way to disguise what's going on in a completely self working masterpiece!

Effect: Several cards are shuffled and laid out in three rows face up. She mentally gets to pick any cards she wants. She never tells you the card. You collect the cards and re-lay them out in three new rows face up. She holds your hand and you feel for energy and try to guess at which row her card is in. She tells you if you are right or wrong. The cards are collected and you try again. The cards are collected and you guess that her card is the eleventh card down in the pile. She deals the cards and you are right!

Secret: The method behind this is that the cards are gathered in a way that always makes her card the eleventh card at the end. How? It takes exactly 21 cards. Make three rows of cards face up. Be sure to lay the cards out the same way each time so you can gather them up from each row correctly. In other words, be sure to overlap the cards onto each within each row as you deal left to right across the three rows until out of cards. There will be three rows containing seven cards. All you have to do to know which card she picked is find out which row it is in twice. The first time you lay out the cards, you will guess which row the card is in. Right or wrong, she tells you which row because you ask if you are right. The cards are gathered up row by row. The secret is that the row containing the card must go in the middle when collecting the three rows of cards and the cards are laid out left to right as you make three new rows! You do this process again. At this point, her card has to be the fourth card from the top of the row that contains her card! Collect the cards again, putting the row that contains her card in the middle. This adds seven cards above her card. This way, her card is always the eleventh card!

Performance: To hide the fact that you are simply getting her to tell you which row it is and that this is some type of self working math trick, you are going to use your powers to guess where her card is. This guise is perfect. Place out the cards, have her pick one, gather them and re-lay out the rows. When laying out the three rows, be sure to lay them out first row, second row, third row, first row, second row, third row until you are out of cards. Instead of asking which row it is in, say that you are going to use your energy to locate her card. Have her hold your hand for a connection. Look like you are concentrating and just take a guess. If you are right, she will freak out. If you are wrong, she will be anxious when you try again. It doesn't really matter. Have her tell you and do it all again. The next phase of laying out the cards automatically locates the card. The card is the 4th card in whichever row she verifies. Put all the cards together with the selected row in the middle and tell her that you think it is the 11th card. Let her deal them. There doesn't seem to be any explanation at all because she never told you the card. This is simple and powerful ice-breaking magic that is intimate and intriguing in it's design.

Tip: Instead of telling her that the cards is the 11th card, deal cards onto the table as if you are still picking up energy. Deal them face down until you "feel" something at the 11th card.

Profiler

Sure, you could spend 20 years mastering micro expressions and body language to pull off "lie detector" tricks or demonstrations of body language. You're in luck. Using the *One-Way* secret or a card force, you could do it today! One of my favorite tricks is determining what someone is thinking. Today, you will be able to pull off one of the greatest tricks of all times with no practice and knowledge of advanced magic!

Effect: A card is chosen by a spectator and placed back into the deck. The deck is shuffled. The magician proceeds to flip cards over while asking questions and "watches for shifts in eye movement, breathing patterns, body position", etc. The guy seems to struggle but takes an educated guess and is right again and again and finally nails the correct card! Dang, that guy is good at reading people!

Secret: Force a card, have it placed back into the deck and shuffled. You might want to spread the cards on the table face up to see how far from the top the card is. I'd recommend cutting the cards or shuffling the cards to get the chosen card toward the top. Otherwise, this might last a little too long! (This trick can easily be accomplished with the *One-Way* principle as well. See Magic Techniques. It's your choice.)

Performance: With the popularity of poker tells and shows with body language experts solving crimes, the popularity of psychology is amazing. You are going to "bluff" them into thinking you are a body language expert! Don't worry, this is easy. You already can find the card with ease because you either forced their card and know what it is or it is marked. Starting from the top, turn cards over one at a time and show them to the spectator. As you show them each card, actually observe their face and make up comments about anything that you see. You know that the card you are holding is not their card, so say something like, "Mmm, I can see that you are breathing normally and there was no change in your eye dilation... I am guessing this is not your card." At the next card say something like, "Ah, you blinked. That's a nervous tension release. You must be trying to throw me off." Continue to play with them until you reach their actual card, which you identify from the one-way marking on the back. Here's the fun part. You know when it is their card and when you hold it up you will most likely see a real reaction of some sort! You can mention that real reaction and make up something about how it reveals their chosen card. If you do not pick up on reaction, you can just say something like, "Ah! Your attempt to freeze up and reveal nothing to me makes me suspicious about this card! This must be your card!"

Tip: Now to really make this a profiling effect, ask them to lie to you as you show them cards. Have them say if a card is or is not theirs. However, you will know for certain if they are lying or not! Play it all off accordingly.

Telethapy

People are almost more amazed with tricks that have no moving parts - like mind reading, for example. Here's a good guise for you.

Effect: A card is chosen and, using "telepathy", the magician is able to reveal the correct card.

Secret: Have the deck prepared according to the *One-Way* principle. With the deck face down, have a spectator legitimately pick any card they want. While the card is in their hand, instruct them to remember it. Meanwhile, rotate the pack end for end and then have the card returned anywhere in the deck. At this point, you can easily find the card by looking for the reversed card back!

Performance: Once the chosen card is placed back into the deck, it is obviously easy to locate it. The real issue is how do you reveal the card without simply spreading the deck, finding the marking and removing the card! This guise might be something you want to try out. Tell them that you have "telepathic abilities," and you want to test them out using some cards. Once they have their card in mind, really have them concentrate on it. Continue in a fashion similar to any of the *One-Way* tricks previously described and locate the chosen card. Perhaps, you could turn the cards one at a time toward you as if you are tying to match the image you had from when they were concentrating. Take cards, one at a time off the top of the deck. Hold the card facing you, with the back toward them and have them think hard about their card. It will be easy enough to know when their card comes up! Eventually, you will come to their card and you can say you are getting "a very strong impression!" Or, make up your own "telepathic" method and patter.

Tip: It will actually make the effect more believable if you struggle a bit and almost make mistakes along the way.

Contact Reading

There is an advanced and legitimate art called Contact Reading, and it is one of my favorite types of magic. Here, I teach you a very clever way to simulate Contact Reading, seeming as though you can pick up subtle muscle indictors in the body to locate any object.

Effect: A card is selected and lost into the pack. The cards are spread out along the table and the magician instructs the spectator to reach out and point down at the cards with their pointer finger. The magician lightly grabs hold of the wrist and guides the arm back and forth above the the cards. The magician seems to pick up on subtle muscle resistance that helps locate the chosen card, and then he drops the spectator's finger directly on top of their selected card!

Secret: Have the deck prepared according to the *One-Way* principle. With the deck face down, have a spectator legitimately pick any card they want. While the card is in their hand, instruct them to remember it. Meanwhile, rotate the pack end for end (with any method) and then have the card returned anywhere in the deck. At this point, you can easily find the card by looking for the reversed card back!

Performance: To mimic Contact Reading, the spectator would have to know where the card is, so it makes sense that the cards will be spread out face up. Therefore, using the marking, go through the cards and cut the cards bringing the chosen card to the top of the deck with deck and chosen card face down. (Or discover their card any way you want. It is reversed and easy enough to locate.) Turn the cards face-toward your self and say, "If I was to pick a card among all of these cards and I picked, lets say the Ace of Hearts, and hid it somewhere, a highly trained expert could actually feel for tension in my muscles that would guide them right to my card! It is a science called Contact Reading. Some of the best magicians in the world can barely do it... I was shown a couple techniques I want to try on you." Meanwhile, you just peeked at what their card is - the top card! Memorize it. Now you can have them shuffle the cards and spread them face up across the table. Take their wrist and have them point down toward the cards as you "float" their pointing hand over the cards. Spot their card while you patter about the changes you feel in their muscles based on how close you are to the card.

Tip: Do not look directly at their card, but spot it out of the corner of your eye. This really amplifies the effect. Now locate their card, set their finger right on top of it, take credit and have fun! It is fun to try and see if you really can pick up their muscle tension. Two things are likely to happen: either, the spectator will slightly push you toward the card; or, they will try to keep you away from it! See what you notice!

Counting Mystery

Effect: A volunteer cuts a deck of cards several times, then counts off the top thirteen cards. On command, each card appears in order and in the same suit - for the full suit! The magician sets the deck of cards face up on the table and asks a volunteer to cut the deck and complete the cut. And again. And perhaps again, if the spectator would wish. The volunteer then counts off 13 cards and set the rest of the deck aside. Taking the pack of 13 cards in hand, the spectator counts to a card by spelling A - C - E, and deals the next card face up - which is mysteriously the ace! Then they count out T - W - O, and deal the next card, which, amazingly enough is the two! Continue counting the entire pack, and place a card after each count: T-H-R-E-E, F-O-U-R, F-I-V-E, S-I-X, S-E-V-E-N, E-I-G-H-T, N-I-N-E, T-E-N, J-A-C-K, Q-U-E-E-N and K-I-N-G!
The entire pack counts out to every card!

Secret: The secret is in setting up the deck before the trick. By ordering the deck in a precise way, the trick works itself! Get your deck of cards, and set them up this way:

1. Separate the cards into the four suits. So, you'll end up with four piles of 13 cards each.

2. Order each suit as follows: 5 - 9 - 10 - K - J - 2 - 4 - 6 - Q - A - 7 - 8 - 3. Order these face up, from bottom to top, so that the three is on top, face up.

3. Place all four packets together. Your deck is all set.

Performance: Place the deck face up on the table. When you have the volunteer cut the deck, have them keep cutting the deck (and completing the cut) until a three is on top. (If they have cut the cards three of four times and you still don't get a three showing, you can take the deck yourself and say, "I'll give the deck one last cut," and casually cut to a three.) Then, take the deck and hand it to them face-down. Have them count off the top 13 cards from the top and set the rest of the deck aside. The cards they count onto the table should go onto each other naturally. (This reverses the order of those cards so the trick will work!) They now should be holding the pack of thirteen cards face down in their hand. Instruct them to count out the word ACE by placing the top card under the bottom of the pack and saying "A". (Keep the card face down during this). Then, repeat for C then E. Then have them deal the next card face up on the table, and amazingly, it's an ace! Now they continue with the cards left in their hand for the number TWO. "T" and it goes to the bottom face down. Then they say "W" followed by "O". The next card is turned face up onto the other card on the table. It's a two! Repeat for all the cards in the pack! Practice it a couple of times yourself before doing it for your friends. If you really want to add professional magic to the trick, come up with a story about the cards and how they can order themselves magically. Your story can be about anything you like: maybe ghosts? Trained cards? Magnets in your hands? You can be creative and build a cool patter that will enhance the trick with your own style.

Tip: The remaining cards of the deck are still set up and ready to repeat if desired!

Magic Tricks with Money

Money Transformation

Effect: A larger bill is borrowed and folded in quarters. You unfold it and it has changed into a one dollar bill!

Secret: Your spectator cannot tell that you have a dollar secretly hidden and folded to begin with.

Performance: There are many advanced methods of doing effects like this. This is by far the easiest and cleanest to start. To start, take a dollar and hold the ends apart in front of you. Fold the dollar left to right in half. Now fold the dollar toward you and down in quarters. Finally, fold the dollar left to right again. Hide this folded dollar in your right hand by your two

middle fingers. You should be able to hold the folded dollar at the first knuckle bend and the base of your middle fingers. When you borrow a five, ten or twenty from someone, you are going to hide your folded bill on the backside of their bill. To do this, reach forward with your right hand face down and grab their bill with your fingers on top. This will automatically add your bill to the top of their bill. Pinch the two bills together with your thumb as you slide the bill toward you. Turn your hand

face up to show their bill. Your folded bill will be hidden under-neath. Place your left finger tips onto the bill at the point where your right thumb holds. Release your thumb and grab the bills with your left finger tips and thumb. The left thumb grabs un-derneath both bills. Turn your left hand up to display their bill to

them. You have now put your bill on your side of their bill in the fairest way possible! Fold their bill toward your left hand out-wardly while keeping your folded bill behind your fingers and their bill. Your fingers will adjust to let the bill fold in half. Now fold their bill forward, downward and away from you in half again. Keep your bill lined up so it does not stick out from the

top or bottom at this point. Fold their bill in half left one more time away from you to essentially match your bill. At this point, you can grab both bills as one with the other finger tips if you like. Continue to fold both bills down together for the first time into one small and stiff length. Unfold this tiny packet from the other side which reverses the bills. You now have your bill on the front and their bill on the back. Unfold only the front, undoing what you did to begin with! Once the One is unfolded, slide their bill off from the back into your fingers and drop the One on the table. Bring your hand down out of site and hide their bill!

Tip: If you want to take this to another level, you can show their bill front and back while you hide your folded bill. Before you fold their bill, you can slide your folded bill from right thumb to left thumb behind their bill easily! You can even open their bill and flip it long ways front to back a couple times. Your bill is easily hidden in back with either thumb tip.

Torn & Restored Dollar

Effect: You borrow a dollar, rip it into quarters and unfold it to find it restored.

Secret: You have a dollar hidden and folded to switch during the ripping and folding.

Performance: Become familiar with the "Money Transformation" effect. This is the same handling, but instead of folding

their borrowed bill up, you are tearing it into quarters before the final folds and flip! In addition, instead of two different bills,

use two dollars so it seems like you tear up their One and fix it magically! You have your dollar hidden and borrow a dollar. It will certainly look like you tore and restored their dollar.

Torn Corner

Effect: A borrowed dollar is folded in quarters and a piece is clearly torn off. You grab the sides of the bill and pull, making the dollar whole again.

Secret: The dollar is never missing a piece but just appears to be by the way your fold and tear.

Performance: Borrow a dollar and fold it in half. Fold it one more time into quarters. It makes no difference in this particular dollar effect which direction or ends you start folding with. Once it is folded into quarters, locate the corner that was originally the center. If you were to unfold the bill, it would be where the creases intersect. Hold the folded bill with that edge with your right thumb and first finger. Actually rip that corner piece about a half inch in from the edge. You are ripping the longer length of the bill. Rip it forward and then bend it backwards and bend that piece behind the dollar. Continue your actions as if you ripped that piece completely off. What you are really doing is keeping that piece held flat and bent over on the back side of the dollar and ripping off nothing. You might position that piece behind the rest of the dollar and secure it with the other thumb. Give a nice snap to the dollar to simulate that you tore off that corner by flicking your thumb nail across the missing area. Pretend to place those pieces in your pants pocket. Displaying the dollar that looks like it has a large chunk out of it, find the edge on the short ends and pull the dollar open. The folded piece will unfold and restore the dollar. Upon close inspection, you'll see that there is just a small line in the dollar. Hold it carefully stretched out and casually for someone to see and put it away like it was no big deal.

Impossible Penetration

Effect: You show a dollar and borrow a business card or piece of paper. The dollar is folded in half and the card is placed folded on the outside. A pen or pencil clearly is shoved through the dollar and paper. However, when the pencil is removed, there is no apparent damage at all even though the paper has a hole in it.

Secret: There is a special slit in the dollar but how it is folded makes it look like the pencil legitimately travels through the center.

Performance: At home, get a dollar and put it on a cutting board. With a razor blade, carefully cut around the innermost half of the circular seal on the left side of the face of a dollar. On the inside of the black seal containing a large letter, cut the

half that is closet toward the left end. When the bill is folded in half, a pencil can pass into the slit and along the back of the bill. However, from the front of the bill, it will look like the pencil is pacing right down the center of the bill. Now that you have your bill gimmicked, there is another set up to do when you do this trick with someone. Find your dream-girl and show her your bill. The position of the opening is perfect to hide with your finger. Fold the bill in half. Also, fold down about an inch or so of the non gimmicked side of the dollar. Crease this part.

Take a piece of paper and fold over the entire bill from under the part you have folded down and the back up high enough to cover the slit you made at home. Once you have this figured out, you can create quite an illusion. Stick a sharpened pencil into the slit from the inside of your folded bill. The pencil will come out the back of the slit and be driven behind the bill as you press the pencil through the paper! Right before you you push the pencil all the way though, you are able to show both sides. Hold your thumb and fingers on each side to press the sides closed to hide the secret. Let them see how fair this all looks otherwise. You can even let your lucky lady push it

through and break the paper. It will look 100% real from all sides! Pull the pencil out and show that the bill is still fine by holding toward the ends of each side of the bill. Nobody would ever suspect a hole toward the edge and will only be looking at the center.

Tip: If you use a business card for this, fold the business card with 1/3 of a distance instead of in half. Put the smaller part on the front side toward the spectator and the long side on the back to cover beyond the hole the pencil will travel through. This is so you can show both sides and hide the hole in back right before you puncture all the way through.

Happy or Sad

Effect: You tell someone that money comes with a hologram built in. You show them. By tilting the dollar up or down, you can clearly see the face frown and smile.

Secret: There is a special fold in the paper to create the illusion.

Performance: To set up this effect, you need to prepare a dollar. It only takes a couple seconds. Lightly fold a bill down the center of a president's face. Try to make it travel through the

midway point of the mouth. In some bills, this will be the center of the bill. In others, it will not. Do not focus on the proportions of the bill, but rather making sure you center the mouth. With the bill folded, the face should be on the inside of the bill. Open the bill back up. Now look at the bottom of the bill where the fold you made meets the bottom of the bill. From this point, you are going to make two final folds. Folding the opposite direction of the original fold, from the point on the bottom through the left eye, make a fold. Do the same for the other half of the face. You will end up with three folds. One through the mouth and two more through the eyes to the middle fold on the bottom. You will see a slight "V" in the face folded one way and a line up the middle folded the other way. Pull on the ends of the bill to flatten it out. Tilt the bill forward and backwards and notice the illusion!

Tip: You can make the folds light so it is not obvious what is going on. Just the slightest combination of these folds will give the illusion you are looking for.

Mind Reading Tricks

Mind reading must be the most interesting things for a girl to experience from a stranger. Without spending a lifetime mastering suggestion and reading people, here's a fantastic way to fake it in minutes!

Miscall

Effect: A girl is handed two books. She picks one and you keep one. You flip the pages of your book and she tell you where to stop. The page number is given and she looks the page up in her book and remembers a word or picture. You then proceed to draw or tell her the exact thought!

Secret: You force the page number in a clever way and already know what word or picture to direct her to on that page.

Performance: Take a couple magazines or books that are laying around the bar or party. Open towards the middle of one and find a good picture on a page that stands out or a good and long word at the top line that stands out. Remember whatever page this is on. We will call this magazine or book "A". Now you can present "A" and "B" together to some girl and ask them to pick one. If they say "A", hand it to them and keep "B" and say, "You take the one you picked." If they say "B", leave "A" on the table and say, "Okay, we will use this one that you picked." Either way, you end up with "B" in *your* hand. Riffle the pages toward you and ask them to say stop. When they do, call out the page number of the secret forced word or picture from "A" no matter what page you are on! This is a total bluff, but nobody will notice because there is no reason to be skeptical yet. Instruct them to take "A" and go to the page they just "selected". This is an easy way to get them to "freely" go to a page you want and pick something you want. Guide them to whatever it is that you have memorized. For instance, "Are there text and articles on this page or just pictures? Oh, there are words. Great. Go to the top line and think of a long word and close the book so I cannot see." Of course, it will be the word you made them pick. If you have seen a magician do advanced effects with this type of material, you'll know how insanely impressive it is. Of course, with this easy method and no skill, you can't go wrong! Lucky you!

Tip: To even enhance the experience more, draw whatever it is they are thinking of. This will be easy since you already know but it will seem even more impossible if you draw their own thoughts!

Elephant in Denmark

Effect: A girl picks a number in her head and is asked to do simple math with her number. Then she is asked to think of a country, animal and color of that animal. Then you are able to tell her what it is.

Secret: Because of the simple math trick involved and the choices you give, there is only one common answer of "Grey elephant in Denmark."

Performance: Ask someone to think of a number. After that, you have them add and subtract any numbers you want from their number. You do the same math except you start with zero. After a few basic additions and subtractions, instruct them to *subtract the number they started with*. (This is done at the same rhythm as all the rest of the math so far and not to be made a big deal.) At this point, you have the same number! Continue with any multiplication, division, addition or subtraction at this point to get them to end up with 4. For instance, they start with 3, add 4 and get 7, subtracts 1 and gets 6, add 20 and gets 26, *subtracts their original number* and gets 23, subtracts 3 and gets 20, divides by 2 and gets 10, subtracts 6 and gets 4. You can easily make it up as you go. Once they have four, ask them if their number is between 1 and 26. Of course it will be, but you are just making it look like any number is possible. Tell them to think of the letter that corresponds to their number. Say, "Think of the number that corresponds with your number. For instance, 'a' is 'one', 'b' is 'two', etc, etc." Give them a moment to come up with their letter and have them tell you when they are done. Now have them think of a country that starts with that letter. It will very likely be Denmark. Have them think of their country and think of the second letter of their country. Have them think of an animal that starts with that letter. Say, "Think of an animal large or small that starts with that letter." As you do this, emphasize large with your hands to help push them to pick elephant. Lastly, have them think of the color of their animal. Almost every time you do this, the answer will be "Grey Elephant from Denmark." After they have all their thoughts, look at them funny and say, "This can't be right. Something must have gone wrong. There are no grey elephants in Denmark." This sounds like a lot of work, but this entire trick only takes a minute. You can imagine how easy it would be to use this trick to make your own message with other letters and animals. Have fun reading minds!

Math Prediction

Effect: Several people choose random numbers and enter them into a calculator. One by one they are multiplied together. The final result was predicted by the performer.

Secret: You are able to make many calculators display anything you want after hitting the equals key if programmed ahead of time.

Performance: You are going to force a number by secretly entering it into a calculator before you start. With the iPhone, for instance, this can be done as you are looking at the phone as if you are just figuring it out. Some cheap or simple calculators may not let this work. You need to just try it out. I have found the iPhone to be the best for this effect because you get to borrow a girl's phone and play with it. This is an intimate thing. Of course, you can use any calculator that lets you do the following set up. Some calculators will create a formula for what you are entering. You are going to set up a very simple formula by entering "A prediction number you want to force" "+" "O" "X". For instance, if I wanted to force a prediction of my phone number, I'd enter "8055551234" or whatever the number is, hit the PLUS key, hit the ZERO key then finally hit the MULTIPLY key. (In some scientific calculators, you might have to enter the "(" key after MULTIPLY.) In mathematical terms, you simply have a number plus zero, no matter what is added or subtracted afterwards. Okay, now for the trick. The screen will only display a zero after you are all set up. Put the calculator or phone in plain site and ask for her and several friends to come up with two or three digit numbers. Ask for the first one and enter it in. Add or multiply the next number and so on and so on. After a few entries, ask someone to hit the equals key. The result will default back to your original secret prediction! This lets you get away with a lot of tricks. You might even enter your own number to be forced and at the end of the trick, have her call the number to see what "random" number you guys created. She'll be surprised that you pick up! Now you have exchanged numbers!

1089 Math Trick

Effect: Three random number are chosen by a spectator. Meanwhile, the magician deals three random cards. The numbers are rearranged and subtracted from each other.... then added. The result is found to be the chosen cards by the magician.

Secret: The secret to the math portion of this trick is quite interesting. Instruct your spectator to take any three numbers. You will want to have a note pad and pencil ready. Give an example like 3-4-7 or 6-2-1. Be careful to remind them to make it "harder" and more interesting by making sure all the numbers are different. (In fact, there are some duplicate numbers that can be picked that can ruin the trick! If the numbers are different, it works 100% of the time!) Have them reverse the numbers and subtract the smaller from the larger. Now simply have them reverse the results and add them up. This number would certainly appear to be random, but it is always 1089. (1+0+8+9=18 which is a multiple of 9 principle in mathematics. If that hurts your head, just accept it and do the trick.) The secret to the three dealt cards by the magician also being 10, 8 and 9 is simply "stacking the cards" ahead of time. You can put them on top and execute an *Overhands Shuffle Force* (see Magic Techniques). You could alternatively choose to stack these three cards on top of the deck and have the girl cut anywhere she wants and use the *Criss-Cut Force*. Set the cards up in order of 10, 8 and 9 (with the 10 being the top card) and this trick works itself!

Performance: Bring out a deck of cards, a note pad and something to write with. Tell the spectator you are going to make a marvelous prediction as you shuffle and then deal three "random" cards. Then you ask the spectator to write down their three random numbers (see Effect for all details). Have those numbers reversed and subtract the smaller from the larger. Take the result and reverse them and add them up. The result is 1089. Reveal that you predicted this long ago and reveal that your cards are 10, 8 and 9!

Tip: You can even use the guise that the spectator is able to have their random numbers match the cards you dealt. Sometimes, the spectator enjoys the trick more when they feel like they did something lucky or magical. Of course, you could just do this simple math trick with a calculator or notepad and leave the cards out of it altogether.

Instant Hypnosis

Effect: A group of people are asked to repeat a few key words and it makes it difficult to answer a simple question correctly.

Secret: There is not much of a secret as this is more about conditioning and association of words. Also, a subtle gesture confuses their head!

Performance: Ask several people to play along. Ask them, "Spell the word pot out loud. All of you, spell top. Spell tops. Spell spot. Spell spots. What do you do at a green light?" As you ask this question, you gesture with your arms like a subtle stopping motion in front of you. In fact, to condition them to absorb your hand movements, gesture with every word you have them spell as well. Point to the ceiling for top. Point at your sleeve for spot. Gesture like you are holding a pot for pot. When you ask them about the green light and gesture with a subtle hands out like stop, they will all say, "Stop." Often, you can ask this question again and again until they start to catch on.

Can't Add

Effect: After you give a group a few simple numbers to add up, they cannot come up with the correct answer.

Secret: The arrangement of the numbers conditions people to think in hundreds. The pattern is hard to break. Before moving on and seeing it all come together, write:

```
1000
  40
1000
  30
1000
  20
1000
  10
```

in a column for simple math. DO NOT add them up in any order you want. Start with the first 1000 and add 40. Then add the second 1000. Then add the 30, etc, etc.

Performance: Write 1000 on a note pad. Below it, write 40. Ask what the total is. They will all say 1040. Then write 1000 below the 40 and ask for the total. They will say 2040. Then write 30 below the second 1000. The answer will be 2070 so far. Then write 1000. below the 30. The answer will be 3070. Then write 20 below the 1000. The answer will be 3090. Then write 1000 below the 20. The answer will be 4090. Then write 10. The final answer will be 5000. It is wrong.

Tip: Do not let people simply add the four thousands first then the smaller numbers second. The spacial conditioning will not work if you let them add the number up in any order they want.

Paper Prediction

Effect: A girl writes anything she wants on a piece of paper. The paper is ripped up and burned. You are able to predict what she wrote.

Secrets: When you rip up the paper, you are able to secretly keep the piece with her prediction and look at it while the other parts are burning.

Performance: Get a small piece of paper and draw a circle in the middle. Turn around and ask your girl to draw or print anything she wants in the center. Have her fold it in half so you

can't see. Turn around and fold it in half again so it makes a square. At this point, the prediction is contained in the corner of the paper that is folded up. Three corners will have edges to them and one will be the original center of the paper. The center is easy to locate as it is the area with folds. Proceed to tear the folded paper into quarters. Of course, three stacks of pieces will be blank inside and the corner piece will still contain the message. Place them together in your hand so that you keep the center part with the message on the bottom. Drop all the pieces except the piece with the message into an ashtray

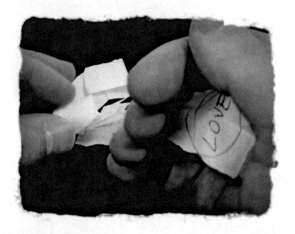

or plate. Proceed to burn what looks to be all the pieces. As they are burning, instruct the girl to visualize her message. Meanwhile, bring your hand down out of site and open up the folded center. You can bring your hand below the table or turn around as you ask her to whisper the message to someone. Peek at the message and discard it. At this point, it is all acting. As the paper stops burning, stare into the smoke and magically come up with her message.

Tricks with Everyday Objects

Ear to Mouth

Effect: Liquid is held in a straw by sucking up some liquid and quickly holding a finger over the end. It is released. Again, it is held back, then the straw is brought up to the ear where it is then released. A second later, the liquid is spit from the mouth into the glass!

Secret: Liquid was secretly held in the mouth the second time liquid was sucked up. Also, the finger didn't actually hold the liquid back the second time. It's a total bluff.

Performance: Taking a straw that cannot be seen through, stick it in a glass of liquid. Hold your finger over the end and lift. Now let your figure go. The liquid falls out. Demonstrate this ability to some girl sitting next to you and tell her that you have a much more advanced version. This time, suck liquid with your mouth and quickly cover the end to get a much greater amount. Release it into the glass. Casually say something out loud to subtly enforce that you do not have anything in your mouth like, "Watch this." Suck up more liquid to fill the straw again. This time, you secretly keep a small mouthful of liquid! Quickly stick your finger on the top of the straw again, but this time do not actually hold tight. Let the liquid fall right out as you lift. Lift the bottom of the straw up to your ear. Lift you finger and pretend to let the liquid release into your ear. Tilt and shake your head like something is happening and spit the liquid from your mouth back into your glass!

Karate Straw

Effect: A dollar is folded lengthwise. A straw is held by a girl and you are able to break it or bend it in half with a folded dollar by coming down onto it like a karate chop.

Secret: The onlookers cannot notice your finger moving to actually do the chopping during the large and fast movement.

Performance: You fold a dollar along its length so you have one thin and long folded dollar. Have someone sitting next to you hold a pencil or straw. Explain that with enough concentration, you can create enough strength and energy in the paper to become powerful. Hold the folded bill at one end by your thumb and first and second finger. Make a couple soft practice line-ups by coming up and down just touching the bill to the object. Then come up very high and come down onto the straw fast. When you come down, quickly point your finger forward and smash through the straw. You will be holding the bill by the thumb and second finger still which allows the first finger to point. After you have penetrated the obstacle, curl your finger back fast and show the dollar.

Suction

Effect: After showing how a straw can hold water by holding the finger on one end and releasing, you say you can do something similar with air. After sucking a little air and putting your finger over the top, you're able to get paper to be sucked up by the straw. When you release your finger, the paper falls.

Secret: When removing a straw from its wrapper, you hold it against the straw as you pull it out to cause static. To release the static, you slightly bend the straw.

Performance: Get a couple of unwrapped straws, unwrap one and use it for demonstration in liquid. Stick it into the liquid and hold you finger over the end to keep the liquid from coming out. Lift the straw then lift you finger to let the liquid fall out. Say to your dream-girl that you can do something similar with just air alone. Take the unopened straw and pull off the very end of the paper. Tear a few tiny pieces from the wrapper end and lay them on the table. Slightly squeeze the the paper just below the rip as you draw the straw out. This will charge the straw well with static. Once set up, be careful not to bend or lay the straw down so you do not loose the charge. Suck a little air into the straw and put your finger onto the end just like you did with the water. This does nothing, but it looks like you might have trapped some air. Bring the straw near the torn pieces and watch as they jump up to the end of the straw. To release them, you want it to look like you just let your finger off the other end. In fact, you do, but you also slightly bend the straw which releases the static. Magic and science at work together!

Spoon and Fork Bending

Effect: A spoon and fork are criss crossed at your finger tips. A moment later, they both melt and are dropped to the table completely bent.

Secret: There is a bend in each before you start but the way it is held appears normal.

Performance: Start by secretly bending a fork and a spoon below their heads. Bend them about thirty to forty-five degrees. With the finger tips of the right hand and thumb, you are going to pinch both the fork and spoon to make them look normal. Do this by laying the back of the bends against each

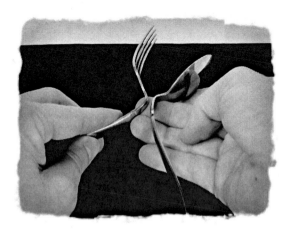

other. Both the head of the fork and the spoon are facing away from you. They are held on their sides arched away from each other and the bend touching. When you place your fingers to hide the "intersection" of the fork and spoon, it will look like

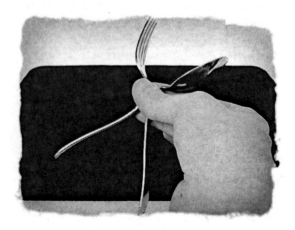

they are simply crossing each other. It is quite a great illusion in itself. Slowly let the pressure of your pinch go and watch the two items look as if they are melting, bending and twisting. A

little acting is needed so concentrate and use your other hand to push energy into the bend. You just created an instant illusion.

Tip: Be sure the handles of the fork and spoon match enough so it is not obvious what is going on. Keep in mind that you could prepare this effect right in front of people by playing with the spoon and fork on the table surface then bringing them both out of sight to your lap. Quickly bend them by pressing each one with each hand against your leg. Hold them by the neck and bend the heads back as you push them onto each leg. One in each hand, they will be bent into place in a second.

Fake Spoon Bending

Effect: A spoon is held by the fist and the head of the spoon is clearly bent back onto the table. The hand is opened and there is no bend!

Secret: It looks like you are bending the spoon when you are not.

Performance: Hold a spoon like you are going to stab the table. Your entire fist surround the handle while the head of the spoon sticks out the bottom. With the curve of the head toward you and slightly down, pull back on the head of the spoon while your fist moves forward. However, you need to let the handle of the spoon fall through all of your fingers except your

pinky. When you push forward, it will look like the handle is being bent forward. The pinky continues to grab around the neck of the spoon to control it.

Tip: Do not let the tip of the spoon handle show out the top of your hands or they will see that it did not bend forward.

Smoking Paper Illusion

Effect: A piece of Zig Zag or cigarette paper is torn up and shown at the finger tips. The pieces are rolled together into a ball then pulled lengthwise like a thin cigarette or joint. The paper is opened to reveal that it has been restored!

Secret: You have an additional ball of paper hidden in your fingers. Also, the paper has a sticky property to it that allows it to stick to your fingers while you spread them.

Performance: Start by secretly taking an additional piece of the paper and rolling it into a ball. Stick this into the bend of your first curled finger. It will hide there well enough. Sit near a girl and show her this trick by removing one of the pieces of paper. Start to tear that piece into smaller pieces. Once you have a few pieces, hold some in each hand at your finger tips. At the same time, roll the hidden ball into that hand's finger tips to join the other pieces. Squeeze firmly and open your hands. All the pieces will stick to your skin and you can amazingly show your hands empty. Using your finger tips, start to manipulate all the parts into one ball being aware of the other rolled, unripped ball. Work the ball of pieces into the bend of your finger and just display the non-torn ball at your finger tips of one hand or just squish the torn ball between the thumb and first finger that you are displaying the new ball with. Start to pull lightly on the side of the ball. Little by little, it will start to look strange that you are pulling a large piece that stays connected to the rest. Continue until you can unravel the entire thing. The torn pieces are easily out of sight still by being hidden in a bend of a finger or pressed between the thumb and first finger which holds the tip of the new restored piece of paper.

Jumping Rubber

Effect: Two rubber bands are shown. One is doubled over and slid deep onto the top two fingers of your hand. The other one is used to twist onto the tips of all the other finger tips of that hand, trapping the other band in the process. You pull up and down to show how firmly secure the top band is. Instantly, the band jumps to the bottom two finger even with a second band twisted along on the finger tips!

Secret: It does not look possible even knowing the secret, but the top band can easily be manipulated to jumping onto the bottom fingers! The real secret is that it is pulled around and not through the fingers as it appears.

Performance: Depending on the size of the rubber bands, you may have to play with this. Using a generic sized office rubber band, loop it over on itself to make it small enough that if you put it on your first two fingers it would not be loose. However, if you pulled on it, you could easily pull a few inches in stretchiness. Start off trying this without the second rubber band. Put it onto the first two fingers all the way to the base. Get your other hand's first finger into the loop and pull up then down towards you to show that it is really on there. After pulling up then down, curl your hand with the band as you pull down along the palm of your hand. While doing this let all of your finger tips sneak into the loop. Keeping the back of your hand

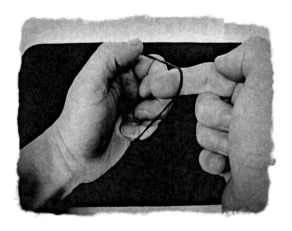

toward the person watching and your palm toward you, everything will still look perfectly normal to them. Do not let them see on top, below or behind your hand. Your thumb can easily hide the extra band on top. Here's the really cool part. Quickly extend your fingers straight again. The rubber band automatically jumps from the top to the bottom! Now you can add the extra part with the second rubber band. Set the first rubber band up as before. With your fingers extended, loop another rubber band onto the tip of the first finger. Twist and put the next finger tip beyond the twist. Twist back. Put the ring finger just past that twist. Twist again and stick in your pinky. Now this will be pretty cool looking. You have a rubber band doubled up onto the first two fingers and another rubber band

locking all the tips of the fingers down. However, if you curl the fingers as you pull the rubber band up and down and stick your finger tips in like before, it will still work! You just have to try this to see for yourself.

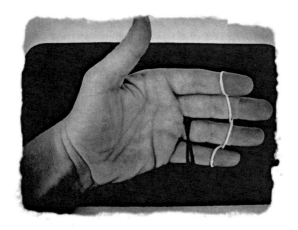

Rubber Penetration

Effect: A rubber band is looped between the right hand's thumb and first finger tip. Across and behind it is another band held by the left hand's thumb and first finger. The bands are pulled by both hands in opposite direction and they are securely locked. Yet, a simple tug and the bands melt slowly through each other!

Secret: This is a little bit of sleight of hand and choreography. The secret is that the bands undo and redo as you stretch them and change a finger position.

Performance: This is a fantastic trick to get down. You will be doing this everywhere you go! It's going to sound confusing, but trust me, it's well worth the time to figure it out. You'll certainly have to practice this a little bit, but you'll be doing it tonight if you get on it. You need two rubber bands that look the same. (For ease of learning, I'm using opposite colors in pictures.)

To start, the size of the band is important. If one is looped over you thumb tip and first finger tip, you should be able to to easily stretch the band as far as you can reach open with your hand, yet it should stay on with your fingers stretched about the width of your palm. If it falls off, it is too loose.

Okay, now that you have rubber bands, here is the holding position for both hands. After getting into the correct holding position, we'll discuss the "move". Hold the right hand as if you were pointing forward. Now, make a large "C" with your thumb and first finger. Your thumb will be pointing toward your left. Loop a band onto the first finger and thumb of the left hand above the knuckles. Hold the left hand as if you were pointing upward. Now, make a large "C" with your thumb and first finger. Loop a band onto the first finger tip. Let it dangle. Let the dangling band go over the backside of the band securely attached on the right hand. Once it is behind the other band, lower it and attach it onto the thumb of the left hand. Stretch the bands on both hands so they do not fall off.

Now you have two bands locked by two hands. If you pulled against each other, they would be pulled or flung off. So, here's how you pull against each other and keep them on. While keeping the bands on each perspective hand, rotate both hands slight upward as in a begging for money gesture. With the fingers all pointing up, you can pull apart and stretch the rubber bands away from each other as seen in the next photo. However, to really get a good stretch, pull to get a little stretch started then pinch the first fingers and thumbs. Your hands are far apart at this point and the fingers of each hand are pinching their one rubber band. This is the exact position

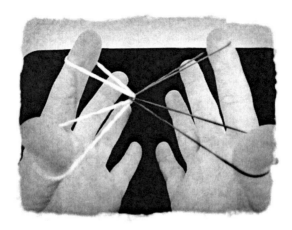

you will eventually switch at! It looks normal and necessary to pull the bands like this. Give the bands a couple good yanks and go back to the regular holding position with both bands held by the "C". Here comes the move. Rotate the hands again, but this time you are going to allow your left first finger to enter the loop around the thumb. When pinching with the left hand, allow the band to come off the first finger and allow the first finger to enter along with the thumb. The middle finger tip will help secure the loop from the first finger that you let go

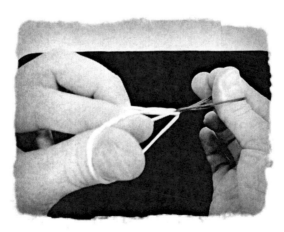

by pinching against the edge of the first finger. Pull and stretch them just like before but be sure to keep pinching so the band doesn't fling off. When you release the stretch, come back to the non pulling position stretch the fingers apart keeping the bands straight. Be sure the left first finger got inside the thumb's loop. The band on the left hand will have flipped from the back to the front of the right hand's band! Push the bands against each other so they still looked linked. Keep massaging the bands into each other so their eyes cannot detect that the bands are apart. It is all acting from this point on. Slowly stop moving as you apparently pull the bands apart. There are many advances and polishes to this that could literally be a chapter on its own. Just give this a shot and think about what you are trying to make this look like. Do it in a mirror and you'll see how to adjust your hands and how dang real this look.

Tip: Once you have this down, let a girl hold one of the rubber bands between her curled first finger of each hand. You then just use your left hand and do the switch move while she holds the other band.

Pick a Finger

Effect: A rubber band is shown. A girl picks a finger and holds it with hers. You attempt to penetrate the rubber band onto the finger she is holding. She shuts her eyes for a second and you do it.

Secret: You ditch the rubber band she saw and grab a hidden band that is already on your arm and up your sleeve.

Performance: Start by having a second matching rubber band placed onto your arm. If you are wearing long sleeves, you can have it just up on the wrist. If you are wearing short sleeves, put it way up the arm out of site. Now you are ready to begin. Tell someone that you are going to do something amazing with a rubber band you have dangling at your finger tips. Put the band on the table and tell them to pick any finger. Tell them to grab the finger they picked tightly so you cannot sneak a rubber band onto it. Take the band and look as if you are trying to saw the band into your skin. Toss it onto the hand a couple times. Even loop it onto other fingers like you are really trying to find a way to penetrate your hand. Finally, explain that they are going to have to shut their eyes for a second. When they do, toss the rubber band over them or drop it and quickly grab the hidden one and pull it down. Pull it onto whatever finger they hand and tell them to look!

Tip: As soon as they look, manipulate the band and make it look like you are still just figuring out the puzzle. On the contrary, depending on the moment, you may want the first image they see to be the band perfectly dangling on the finger they are holding. It's up to you.

Corked

Effect: Two corks or dollars rolled into tubes are held at the base of the notch of the thumb and first finger of each hand. The hands are rotated and the finger tips from the opposite hand grab hold at the ends of the objects. The object certainly appear to be locked inside of each other, yet the hands come apart with the objects between the finger tips.

Secret: The objects are held by the finger tips of each hand and look locked but they are not.

Performance: You do not need any set up for this. Grab a couple dollars and roll them into tubes or grab a couple corks from the bar, party or restaurant. Lipstick and ChapStick® both work great as well. You will place one cork in the notch of each hand. Hold the cork with just the base of the thumb at the palm. The cork will stick out past the top of the hand and also extend into the palm area. To grab hold of all the ends of these items with your finger tips, you are going to rotate your right hand. Hold your left hand comfortably in front of you. Your right hand will rotate up bringing your right thumb to the top. One hand is up and one hand is down at this point. From here, you are going to grab the ends is a weird way that is much easier to explain if you now jump to phase two. Just for learning purposes, remember this position but I want you to take the corks and hold them in each hand between thumb tip and middle

fingers of each hand. Get back to the same up and down position from a minute ago. From the front, stick the left hand's cork into the notch of the right hand. Rotate your right hand forward a bit to get the cork in the right hand's finger tips into the notch of the let hand. Now this is exactly how you will grab the corks when placed in the notches to begin with! Take a good look and remember this mini twister game going on in your hands. You can grab the corks in the notch to get back to the starting position. Release the finger tips and try to grab them again with the corks held in the notch. When done correctly, it will not look so obvious from the front. When someone else tries this, they will not be able to bring their hands apart because they will be linked by the corks.

Stick Penetration

Effect: Two hard match sticks or toothpicks are interlocked by being held by the finger tips and thumbs of both hands. The hands pull against the sticks to show that they are solid and they cannot pass through each other. In plain site, the sticks melt though each other. Then back in. Then back out!

Secret: There is a secret opening immediately behind one of your fingers by a unique set up.

Performance: You can set this up right in front of people. However, there is a secret. First of all, this is easiest with hard match sticks. If using match sticks, the set up is simply putting of your hands in your mouth and breathing heavily onto your thumb and middle fingertip. Next, you immediately press and hold a match stick between those two fingers. Take a second match stick and hold it with the same fingers of the other hand after you put it over the first match stick. You'll end up with one hand with a match stick held at the thumb and middle finger unable to pull freely since it is blocked by the criss crossed stick held by the other hand. Whichever hand that you moistened is the hand that needs to hold the stick level to the spectators eyes because that is the hand containing the secret

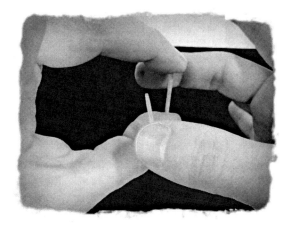

opening. Pull the sticks against each other to prove they are secure. On one of the attempts to pull against each other, slightly open your fingers holding the level stick and you'll see that the base of that stick opens right up as the other end stays stuck to your skin. Pass the other stick through and close the gap. After the passthrough, try to go back and tilt the hands so everything can be seen as normal from other angles.

Go back to the level position and reenter. Come back together and show that they are locked by rubbing and tilting the hands again. It's quite a remarkable trick when done smoothly. Now, if you do not have access to match sticks, round toothpicks work just fine. However, the set up is a little different. Break a toothpick in half and remove the point as close to the end as possible. One toothpick should give you two little sticks. Instead of relying on the moisture of your finger to stick to the head of the match, you are just dealing with wood. To get one end to stick and the other to open in this case, dab the end of one of the sticks on your tongue. Press the sticks very firmly into your finger tips of each hand and wait a few seconds. Open the fingers slightly on the side that contains the licked stick and see which end comes open first. All you are doing is creating a situation for different environments on each end that stick so one will open much easier than the other. The rest is just angles and timing. Remember, keep the side that opens level with the viewer. Do this in a mirror and you'll be amazed that you can open your finger an inch and not tell from a head-on angle. In performance, you only open a tiny bit.

Multiplying Balls

Effect: Three olives are on a plate. An olive (or any small object or paper ball) is placed in the left hand. Then another. The third is placed in a pocket. When the hand is opened, all three olives are back. This is repeated. One to the hand. Then a second. The last olive is clearly and openly eaten. The left hand is opened and there are still three olives!

Secret: There is only one secret extra olive to start with, but they seem to keep multiplying.

Performance: Start by having an olive hidden in your right hand by curling the middle two fingers. Show a dish with three olives or simply grab three from a pile. Show your left hand palm up and place an olive from the three showing onto the palm of the left hand. The left hand closes a little. Another olive is picked up and dropped into the left hand *along* with the hidden olive. This is easily hidden because when your right hand comes down to drop the olive, the fingers block everything. The left hand now curls completely around what is supposed to be two olives. The third olive on the table is clearly picked up and placed into your pocket. However, when you go to your pocket, put it into the original hiding position so you can be all set for phase two. At this point, you can open your left hand and roll out three olives. Start again before there is any time to inspect things. Olive one goes into the left hand. Olive two goes into the left hand *along* with the hidden olive. The third olive is very clearly eaten. Show your right hand open and clean. This is what will be remembered later. Open your left hand to show all three olives again.

Vanishing Pencil

Effect: A coin is placed on a girls hand. You say you are going to make it vanish. With the aid of a pencil as a wand, you wave it over the coin a few times. All of a sudden the pencil has vanished. You both have a good laugh and then you remove the pencil from behind her ear.

Secret: The pencil is hidden behind your ear and out of site of the girl watching.

Performance: Even though this is a trick a grandpa would do on a grandchild, it still creates a nice intimacy with a new female friend. Have a girl hold out her hand and place a coin on it. Tell her that you can make it vanish. Have her close her hand. Stand on an angle so that your right ear is out of site from the girls perspective (Left if you are left handed). Take a pencil and tap the coin. Bring the pencil up toward your ear and back down onto the coin. Do this one more time but this time leave the pencil behind your ear. Come down and say, "It's gone!" You'd be amazed how often they are so focused on the coin that they do not even notice the pencil is gone. Rub your fingers and show that the pencil is gone. Once she realized that the coin is still there and the pencil is what has vanished, there will likely be a large moment of looking away, laughing or reaction. Take a chance to grab the pencil during her reaction and reach towards her ear. Holding the pencil at its extreme tip, drag the pencil along her hair and ear. Once the pencil becomes in view for her, it will appear like it came from far away.

All Shook Up

Effect: Two cans of soda are presented to a girl. She picks one and shakes it up. You tell her you will move the soda to the other can that you have not touched. You open the shaken can and no explosion. You open the regular can and it explodes over with soda!

Secret: Two secrets are at play here. One, when a can is shaken, it can be safely opened in under 30 seconds easily. Two, a non shaken soda can appear to overflow with the correct handling.

Performance: There is no set up required besides being at a party, bbq or picnic with sodas laying around. Present two sodas or have a girl hand you two of her own picking from a nearby cooler. Tell her that you can make the soda from one can travel to the other. To prove it, have her pick one and shake it up. Set the two cans next to each other and gesture as if you were doing something mysterious. Perhaps, place your hand near one and concentrate, then move to the next. After about 25 seconds, grab the shaken can and open it slowly. It will seem strange that it did not overflow. Now turn toward the other can and grab it. Depending on how intensely she is watching, you might give a subtle shake and quick movement with the can to help it burst. In actuality, all you have to do is secretly squeeze the can when you open it. Create pressure by squeezing and opening it up slowly as if it is about to flow all over. When it does blow open and pour onto your hands, she'll be quite surprised.

Unburnt Match

Effect: You bring out a matchbook, open it up, remove a match and light it. The burnt match vanishes and is found burnt and attached inside the matchbook.

Secret: You secretly bend over and burn a match before starting the trick.

Performance: Before bringing out a matchbook, you have to quickly prepare it. Open a matchbook and pull out a few random matches so at the end of the trick there will not just be one spot missing. You also need to burn one match that is attached on the front row of matches. Do this by carefully bending it out of the matchbook and closing the flap over to protect the other match from fire. Be very careful and light this match with a lighter or other match. Let it burn and blow it out quickly before the tip gets too brittle. Once it is cool, bend it back in place and you are set to go. For the trick, bring out the matchbook and open it with the back toward someone. With your thumb, bend the burnt match towards you and keep your thumb over the entire length of the burnt match as you bring down the matchbook for the person to see the rest of the matches. Let them pull out a match. Reverse the process of

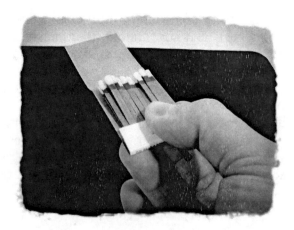

hiding the match by holding the flap up and flipping the entire matchbook flat onto your hand as the match is bent back up into place. Lift the matchbook with the back towards the person with the other hand and close the flap down. Use the back of the matchbook to strike the match she removed and let it burn. Blow it out and shake it a bit. If you want, perform the *Simple Object Vanish* from the Magic Techniques section to make the burnt match vanish. Otherwise, toss it or drop it when you get an opportunity. Perhaps, say, "Grab the matchbook and look inside." As she grabs the matchbook, drop the match and stand on it. Keep your hand in a position as if you are still holding it by your fingers. Gesture with a tossing action toward the matchbook before it is opened up all the way. She will be shocked to see the match still attached and burnt inside the matchbook.

Coin Through Table

Effect: A small glass or salt shaker covers a coin on the table. You cover the glass with a napkin to push the coin through the table. However, the coin stays and the entire glass goes through the table.

Secret: The napkin momentarily takes the shape of the glass that you drop according to the performance.

Performance: While sitting at a table, grab a small glass or grab a salt shaker. Place a coin on the table and tell your new friend that you are going to make the coin vanish or push through the table. Place the glass onto the coin. Next, place a paper napkin or paper of any kind over the glass. Squeeze down on the paper and form the paper around the sides of the

glass. The paper will the take shape of the glass and show that it is covering something. You want to make sure the paper covers the entire side of the glass. Next, concentrate to make the coin vanish. Lift the glass to check your work. You'll both see that the coin is still there. However, what you are really doing is bringing the paper and glass towards the edge of the table and dropping it in your lap! This is done casually and easily as you lift to peek at the coin.

Place the empty paper mold of the glass back down onto the coin. Remove your hand. It will look just like the glass is still sitting there. Smash down the paper hard with one hand while grabbing the glass from your lap from the other. Click the glass underneath the table and bring out the glass. Say, "Wow! The entire glass went through the table. I must have pushed too hard!"

Karate Finger

Effect: A sugar packet is tossed into the air and your finger plunges right through it to stop it in mid air.

Secret: There is a second packet already hidden in your curled hand.

Performance: While sitting next to the girl you want to impress or surprise, grab an extra sugar packet from the table. From below the table and out of site, tear a small hole in the middle of both sides and shove your right first finger through it. Curl this back to hide it as best as possible. You are all set to start the trick. Ask the girl to grab a sugar packet for you. Take it with your left hand and toss it into the air. Immediately catch it in your right hand. Catch it in a closed hand like you normally would except extend your first finger in mid-catch as you drive your hand forward. It will look like you speared the sugar packet with your finger!

Tip: *If you are not sitting next to a girl, you can simply approach her and say, "You dropped your name tag", show her the "sugar" packet and continue the trick.*

Appearing Drink

Effect: While sitting at a table, you mention to the girl that you want to refill her bottle. A cloth napkin is drawn across the bottle and there her bottle is instantly filled.

Secret: There is a clever way of holding the napkin and clipping a full bottle held in your lap.

Performance: Imagine you are sitting across the table from a girl. Their bottle of drink is empty. Tell her you would like to get her a refill. To prepare, have a new bottle of drink held between your knees below the edge of the table. If you extend your toes or lift your legs, you should be able to bring the bottles neck above the table edge. For now keep the bottle hidden below the table edge from her angle. Proceed to take a cloth napkin or towel and hold it by the two outer corners with your thumb and first fingers. Extend it open and create a wall between the empty bottle and the girl. As you do this, let your right hand's pinky and ring finger clip the neck of the empty bottle. At the same time bring the top of the cloth close enough to let the left hand's pinky and ring finger clip the neck of the

awaiting new bottle. Of course, you have now lifted the new bottle up with your legs so you have not apparently moved your hands very much. At this point, all she sees is you quickly covering her bottle and dragging the top of the curtain toward you a bit. Lift up the new bottle onto the table as you adjust the napkin up and forward again. At the same time, drop the old empty bottle onto your lap. Immediately pull back and down on the napkin to reveal the new bottle. Be sure to place the bottle in the same position and direction the old bottle came from.

Ring and String

Effect: A girl's ring is put on a string, tied to your hand and it vanishes.

Secret: You are able to secretly slide the ring off the string when you ask her to tie a knot.

Performance: Using someone else's object makes a trick much better. Borrow a girl's ring. The bigger and heavier the better. You will also need to have a shoe string or thin cord, string or rope about two feet long. Have her slide the ring onto the string and hold up the ends of the string with each hand. The ring will dangle in the middle. Place your right hand over this ring like a downward fist. To make the trick easier in a moment, let the ring be a little more towards your pinky side of your downward palm when your grab hold. Tell her to let go of the string ends. They will fall and dangle downward off each end of your hand. With your left hand, take the left string and pull it up and over the back of your hand to the side of the opposite end. Here comes the secret move. Reach over your right hand with your left hand and grab the long dangling string with the entire left hand in a fist. As you do this, tilt the right hand, thumb up, to allow the ring to fall out of the right hand

into the left hand. Pull the ring along with the left hand as you apparently just pull the string over the top of the right hand. Pull the ring all the way off the end of the string secretly. What it looks like you have done is reach over, grab the other dangling string and pulled it over the back of the right hand. You have created an "X" with the ends of the strings on the back of the hand. Now you instruct her to tie a knot on the string "so the ring can't come off." As she does this, you can ditch the ring nearly anywhere. I sometimes stick it on my pinky finger of my left hand. As she finishes, grab her hand and place it on your wrist with your left hand and tell her to hold tight so you can't cheat. After a moment of looking like you are struggling with your right hand, wiggle your left fingers to show her the ring! If you have stashed the ring in a pocket then look like you are struggling to get the ring off from inside the right hand and say, "You know, I'm having trouble getting the ring off because it is in my pocket." Have her reach in your pocket (Ah, the perks of tricks) and get the ring.

Palm Ashes

Effect: A girl holds a closed hand out. Ashes are rubbed onto the back of her hand. You rub the ashes away. When she opens her hands, the ashes are found inside her hand!

Secret: She does not know you placed ashes in her hand before the trick was on its way.

Performance: Tricks that are mysterious and let you touch or be touched make for great connections. To prepare for this mystery, you need to have access to ashes or create some. You can either use ashes from a nearby ashtray or create some from a trick that requires you to burn up paper. You will need to dab your middle finger of your right hand into the ashes before this trick starts. Also, you will need to have the ashes available during the trick. Now you are set.

While sitting next to your future wife, ask her to hold out her hands flat in front of her. Without much attention brought to it, grab both of her hands and grab them with your thumb on top and your middle finger below and gently wipe the ashes onto her palm of her left hand. You are doing this as you slightly bring her hands a little closer as an excuse to touch her. This action is subtle and should not be a big deal. You are no longer touching her. Ask if she is right or left handed. If she say "left", tell her that you will use the left hand. If she says "right", tell her to take her right hand and rub the back of her left hand. Either way, her left hand (which has been marked below) is still outreached. Have her close her hand tight. Using the same ash finger, dip it into the ashes. Bring that finger to the top of her left hand. Rub a tiny amount of ash onto her hand. Tell her to concentrate. Tell her that she will feel something in her hand. Start rubbing the ashes away. This is very powerful because she does not know what is about to happen. You've told her that "something" is about to happen in her hand. Now tell her that she should start to feel a tingle or some warmth. Well, kinesthetically, it will happened have naturally and they will likely admit to feeling something! Regardless, rub the ashes away, let her go and tell her to look in her hand. The ashes will apparently have traveled into her hand.

Origami Butterfly

Effect: A bill is transformed into a butterfly with actual moving wings!

Secret: The bill has a very unique pre-fold in it. Also, the slight pinch with your fingers makes the wings flap.

Performance: This takes a bit of preparation and folding. Once you do it a couple times, it is quite easy. Just follow the steps exactly and have a blast making girls smile with this classic gem.

Start by placing a bill face up on a surface. Be sure it is orientated with the top away from you so you can read the words normally. Fold the entire bottom away from you, making one long half bill. Line up the edges of the top and crease it perfectly with the crease still toward you. At this point, you will have to lift the bill off the table. Fold the right half below the left half exactly in half. Put the packet as is on the table with the main creases toward you. The folds should face toward and the exposed four layers should be facing away from you.

Next, you are folding corner to corner. Imagine a line from the upper right corner to the bottom left corner. Take the top layer by itself and fold it over exactly at the points at the corner. Flip

the bill over and do the same thing for the other side. Open the bill up in the middle and lay it flat on the table. You should have two small triangles showing from underneath pointing towards you. Now you are going to bend both halves of the bill

upward at a right angle like a paper airplane. Do this by starting with the right side. Bend the bottom right triangle upwards until it has flipped over and points towards the left. You should see how there is a crease in the center of the bill as a guide. This is the center fold from step two. Crease it there. You should have an angle on the bottom right of 45 degrees and a straight edge along the top right showing the top left corner of the back of the original bill but rotated 90 degrees clockwise. If this is what you see, then you have done it correctly. Do the opposite side in the same way. This left half's "triangle" will overlap the right half's. You will have a point at the bottom pointing toward you now like an arrow.

From here, flip the folded bill over left to right so the point is

still pointing towards you but it is flipped over. With the next fold, you will start to see the butterfly start to appear. Notice the right side where there is the dollar amount in the right upper corner. Move down the right side until you get to the fold creating a corner. Grab there and bring that corner to the middle of the dollar like an airplane fold again. This half of the butterfly is going to be allowed to flip toward the right and reverse. You are only folding the top two layers. You should see the back of the right half. In other words, the right 45 degree angle is brought toward the middle and lined up directly on the middle fold of the entire bill. If done correctly, you should be able to read the front bottom dollar amount orientated exactly normal. Repeat this type of fold for the left half of the butterfly. You

have the basics of the butterfly! Now, to make the parts that help it animate, flip the entire butterfly over from left to right again. You will have the point in the bottom facing you. To get the tiny folds created to give you the ability to animate the but-

terfly, you are going to have to make a couple of extra fold and guide lines. Looking at the bill as it sits now, you'll see a small little pocket on the center of the bill. You will eventually be pulling this open and towards you. But first, you need to make a couple folds to guide it correctly.

Take the right point of that pocket and bend it right and down to line up in the center of the bill like another airplane fold. You will be folding the two small layers over here. Crease here and fold it back. Do the same for the left side. Reach into the pocket and you'll notice another little layer of folds making a point inside. Grab that layer that is hidden and the top of the pocket and pull it towards you and down. You will see how all these little folds start to work. You want to get the point you are pulling towards you and down to come as low as possible and the edges close up on the fold you made. You should see the edge of the mouth closing as you push the parts into place. It's a lot of tiny parts trying to come together and you'll have to manipulate each half to line up on the center line and close that opening which runs perpendicular to you.

Once done, on the most center of the entire bill, you'll see a flap or tongue that can bend forwards and backwards.

You have made a little triangular tab that you will eventually grab with your finger tips to animate the butterfly. To make the butterfly work, press you first finger tip and thumb tip tight into the base of this flap and squeeze! You'll see the butterfly wings flap. When performing this, you do not want to have a lot of obvious movement with your fingers. Practice this in a mirror and see how beautiful it is. You'll soon see that holding the butterfly at an angle in flight looks much more real.

Tip: You can have the folds all done and unfold the bill when you sit next to someone. By holding the pre-folded bill by the center edges just above the center fold and facing away from you, use your fingers to push the bottom half away from you. Push your fingers toward each other and the bill will begin to fold into a butterfly by itself. You slightly help the bill come up and fold onto itself toward the spectator, but it is fairly self working. Once you fold the bottom half up, re-grip the bill from the bottom edges or triangles to help rotate the middle section onto itself. You'll see the flap that you hold to animate bend down onto itself. Use your thumb to help close this up. It's like magic!

Napkin Flower

Effect: A paper napkin is transformed into a rose.

Secret: There is a simple way to fold the napkin to create a rose, stem and leaf.

Performance: This is another wonderful gift and ice-breaker. Take a paper napkin and hold the left upper corner with the back of your left first two fingers facing her. Your thumb is on your side of the napkin in the left upper corner of the napkin. Hold this level with your right hand adjusting the right upper corner. Hold tight with your left hand so your right hand can become free. You are going to use the right hand to help wrap the napkin around the left two fingers like a tube. Your left fingers are held pretty deep to give you something to wrap around. Wrap the napkin up and away from you by grabbing the bottom and bringing it around. Go over the top and wrap the napkin completely around the left fingers. After a full rotation, use the right hand to pull on the opposite end of the tube

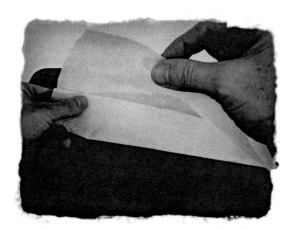

to keep it straight. Use your left thumb to keep the tube from unrolling or falling off. You are not rolling this very tight. Keep it comfortable as you are going to need a little slack to manipulate the paper in a moment.

Once you have the tube, hold it vertically and grab about two inches or so from the top by the sides. With the finger tips of

both hands, press the tube together here like you are choking the tube. Pinch the left thumb and first finger to keep the tube collapsed about two inches below the top as you roll this part of the tube counterclockwise as if you were looking down the top of the tube. The right hand twists just below this point in the opposite direction. Twist until about one third to one half of the length below is twisted into a tight stem. This will leave enough below to make a leaf and more stem below. Find the portion below that is the corner edge of the napkin. This will be pulled up to create the leaf. Pull it up and out slightly unrolling

a bit to give a couple inches of a leaf. Once you've done this once, you'll easily see how much you prefer to make the right sized stem, leaf and rose. Once you have a portion of that corner pulled up and outward, pinch the rest of the napkin below the leaf and twist the rest of the stem in the same direction as you did above. So, by pinching just below the leaf with the left thumb and first finger, roll the stem again as the right fingers twist the opposite way below. If you go the wrong way,

you will unravel the stem. Once done, tighten the entire stem by grabbing the bottom by the right fingers and the top, just below the rose head, with the left fingers and twist it all tight. Adjust the leaf and make it look better if need be. To make the flower head appear a little fuller and beautiful, hold the neck again with the left finger tips and push your right fingers deep into the the head. Push outward at the bottom to bring out the differentiation from the head and the stem twisted tight below.

Finally, while still holding the neck with the left fingers, grab the most inside fold of the flower head with the right finger tips. This is the part inside the top you see twisted like a tube. Grab the most inside corner and twist the entire rose in the opposite

direction to make the rose pedals fuller and more distinct. You are taking the loosely rolled paper and slightly tightening and separating the layers to create the final rose pedals that swirl around in the head of the flower.

Bar Bets

The Perfect Card Bet

Oh, it is rewarding sometimes to set people up! This is a great bar-bet that you can't loose.

The Bet: A spectator picks a card, puts it back in the deck. The magician turns cards face up and places them on the table, each time probing to find out if that was the chosen card or not. The magician obviously does not know what they are doing as they pass right by the chosen card! Then the magician says, "I'll bet you $10 that the next card I turn over will be your card!" The spectator takes the bet because they know that the magician already blew it and passed their card! Then the magician smiles and simply turns the chosen card, which has been passed, back over face down from where it lay on the tabled card pile!

Secret: Have the deck prepared according to the *One-Way* principle (See Magic Techniques). With the deck face down, have a spectator legitimately pick any card they want. While the card is in their hand, instruct them to remember it. Meanwhile, rotate the pack end for end (with any method) and then have the card returned anywhere in the deck. At this point, you can easily find the card by looking for the reversed card! I'll mention here that you can do this scam just as easily by forcing the card if you choose.

Performance: There is not much to this bad boy! After the card is placed back into the deck, it will be a cinch to located as you turn each card over onto the table one at a time. The back of the cards will slowly reveal themselves and there is no real worry. If you notice the card was returned to the deck towards the bottom, you know you will have a lot of cards to turn over! You might consider cutting the deck to bring the card closer to the top. This will not affect the secret if you keep the cards facing the same direction when you cut (or shuffle). A good tip is to lay the cards across each other as they are turned face up onto the table so you can see them all easily. When you come to the chosen card with the reversed image, you know that is their card. Be sure to remember this card once you turn it face up onto the table! Continue with a few more cards, then stop. While holding the next cards, act like you have a hunch the next card is going to be their and offer the bet! They will take it. Then simply put the card you are holding back onto the pack, reach back down to the table and turn over their card you spotted moments earlier! You said, "I'll bet you that the next card I turn over will be your card!" and you were right!

The Kissing Bet

The Bet: You bet that you can kiss a girl without touching her in any way.

Secret: You loose the bet on purpose.

Performance: Tell the girl that you will bet her a dollar (or a drink if appropriate) that you can kiss her without using your lips, tongue or touch of any kind. Girls are usually suspicious so it may take some sweet talking. If the girl doesn't take the bet, say that you want to show her a trick she can use to make money off people. Act as if you're doing her a favor by showing her this! Then if she accepts, do the trick. Move in like you are going to kiss her on the lips. Get close with your hands but do not touch her. When you reach the point of no return you absolutely must lay the smoothest kiss on her she has ever experienced. Then say "Wow! You're a good kisser! Dang it. I lost that bet. I owe you a buck!" A good line here, if appropriate, is "I don't think that kiss was worth a dollar, you owe me another!" Of course, this is said in a funny tone that lets her know that this isn't the end of the world and that you have a great personality.

On Edge

The Bet: The bet is getting a paper match to land on its side.

Secret: You bend the match.

Performance: Grab a paper match out of a matchbook. Demonstrate dropping it onto the surface. Make a bet that you can drop it and land on it's side in one drop. Explain that you will not touch it once it lands and will drop it from the distance demonstrated. Let them try it a few times. Once the bet is on, bend the match into a slight "L". It will now land on its edge when you drop it.

Coin Cross

The Bet: You have displayed a cross of coin or bottle caps. There is a row of four and a row crossing of three. It looks like a cross. Bet that only one coin can be moved to make two rows of four.

Secret: People do not think in three dimensions. You stack one of the coins in the middle!

Performance: Lay out four coins or bottle caps away from you. At the second to the top coin, lay another coin on each side. You essentially make a cross. One row has four coins and the other row has three coins. Bet them that you can move only one coin and make two rows of four. Upon studying, the bet will be taken. It is quite simple when you move the extra bottom coin in the row containing four coins and put it in the dead center where the coins cross. Stacking the coins won't enter people's minds very often.

Tip: To enhance painting a picture in their mind down the wrong path, demonstrate when you offer the bet by sliding a coin from one place to another. Do NOT lift any when demonstrating. Get them thinking about moving them so they have a mental block when evaluating the bet and possibilities.

117

Turn Around

The Bet: Ten coins make a triangle similar to a set up of bowling pins. There is one in the first row, two in the second, three in the third and four in the bottom row. The bet is that you can point the entire triangle the opposite direction by only touching three coins.

Secret: There is no real secret except people have a hard time thinking in this sort of spacial way. Sometimes the answer is too simple.

Performance: Lay out the coins with a top coin as the point. Below that, place two coins. Below that place a row of three coins. Lastly, make a row of four coins. Space them all out so it is even. The three coins that need to be moved are the three on the points of the entire triangle. Take the bottom outside two and slide them to the sides of the row with two coins. This is the second row. Next, slide the top single coin to the bottom!

Drinking Bet

The Bet: Three shots are lined up in front of someone. You have three mugs to drink in addition. Bet that you can drink the three larger mugs before they can drink the three little shots. The rules specify that nobody can make contact with the other person's glasses.

Secret: You trap one of their glasses without touching it by inverting one of yours.

Performance: After you bet that you can drink thee mugs of beer before she can take three little shots, be sure to clarify that nobody can make contact with the other person's glasses. When someone says "go", drink your first mug as fast as you can. When finished, flip it upside down and place it over the final shot of hers. Now she cannot touch it because the rules clearly say that you cannot touch the other person's glass!

60 Cents

The Bet: You can bet they can't tell you which coins you're holding if you tell them the total plus another clue. You state, "There are two coins in my hands that total 60 cents. One of them is not a dime." They can't guess which coins they are.

Secret: It's a play on words that is so obvious that the solution is missed.

Performance: "There are two coins in my hands that total 60 cents. One of them is not a dime." They end up being a fifty cent piece and a dime! When they say that you said that one of them is not a dime, you say, "Correct. This 50 cent piece is not a dime!" You told them clearly that one of them is not a dime. You didn't say both of them are not a dime. It does not get more fair than that.

Roller Bill

The Bet: A bottle has a dollar placed centered over the opening. Another bottle is inverted and placed mouth to mouth sandwiching the bill. You bet that they can't remove the bill without the bottles falling. You are not allowed to touch the bottles.

Secret: You must roll the bill to remove it.

Performance: Set the bottles up with the bill in between and make the bet. When they try several times and fail, take your turn. You can use a pencil or pen to help, but this can easily be

done with just your finger tips. Roll the dollar from one end around itself. Keep rolling until you hit the roll against the bottle mouths. Keep rolling carefully and the bill will be sucked up form the other side into the roll.

Tip: When gesturing during the explanation that they cannot remove the bill, give a tugging motion on the bill to plant the idea of pulling it out fast. Do not hint that you can fold or roll the bill. It helps a lot to throw people of with subtle non verbal cues. It is like saying that you have to pull the bill without actually saying that.

Falling Bottles

The Bet: A bottle has a dollar placed centered over the opening. Another bottle is inverted and placed mouth to mouth sandwiching the bill. You bet that they cannot remove the bill without the bottles falling. You are not allowed to touch the bottles. You are not allowed to roll the bill.

Secret: By holding the extreme end and slamming a finger through the bill, it can be removed. Delicate, slow movements will not work.

Performance: One bottle is balanced upside down on the mouth of another with a bill between them. To remove the bill, you need to hold one end of the bill with your finger tip and slam down with your other hands first finger between where you are holding and where the bottles meet. If someone simply pulls fast, the bottles will fall. If someone pulls lightly, the bottles will fall. If you hold the bill's end and slam your first finger down very fast between the end and the bottles, the bill will be sucked out without the bottles falling.

Geometry

The Bet: Six matches are flat on the table making a triangle and parallelogram. The bet is that they can use the six matches to make four equilateral triangles.

Secret: They are stacked three dimensionally.

Performance: With six matches on the table, move them around to make simple shapes like squares or triangles. Ask someone if they can make four equilateral triangles with just the six match sticks. They will try all sorts of possibilities, but not likely place them like a teepee. To show it can be done,

make a simple triangle on the surface. Take the remaining three matches and stick them in the corners of the triangle on the table with their others ends all together in the center. You've made a pyramid with three equilateral triangles.

Pick up Straws

The Bet: A bent straw and half straw make a pyramid on the table. The bend of the straw is up and the end of the half straw end is propped against it. The bet is that another straw is used to pick up both pieces of the other straws without toppling them.

Secret: There is a clever way to get the straws to lock together without touching them with your hands so they can be lifted as one unit.

Performance: Set up the bet by bending a straw in half. You can use a lighter to help mold and keep the bent straw bent if necessary. Take another straw and cut it in half. Place one of the halves with the end leaning against the middle of the other straw like a tent. In other words, the bent straw has its bend up and is propped against the half straw. When someone tries to pick up the two leaning straws with the left-over half or another straw, they can't. The pieces always fall apart and there will appear to be no way to pick them up together without using their hands. The real trick is to place the lifting straw along side the underside edge of the leaning bent straw. Come in from the side so you can slide your lifting straw along both the legs. Do not go between the legs of the bent straw. Once you are about one third down from the top, push the bent straw

away from the other half straw just a tiny bit. The half straw will fall onto your lifting straw. Now lift and let the half straw lock under the bend instead of leading against it. You can now easily lift the tent as once piece!

It Just Doesn't Measure Up

The Bet: Take a string and glass and bet that the circumference of the glass around the mouth is longer than the height. To make the bet more interesting, add several items under the glass.

Secret: It is amazing how much longer it is around the mouth of a standard beer glass. It is enough to measure many inches longer than the height of the glass!

Performance: First measure with the string to see how tall you can make the glass. Each glass is different, but the beer glasses that are bigger at the mouth than the base are best. It is amazing that you can often stack up 6 deck of cards or several books and still win the bet! Once you know the proportions and how much you can get away with, you can set up the bet. Make the bet more impossible by stacking several items that you know are within your secret measurement and take the bet that the circumference is more that the top of the glass to the table. It will appear impossible.

Olive and Glass

The Bet: Sitting is an inverted wine glass over an olive. The bet is to get the olive into the girl's hand without touching the olive.

Secret: The trick uses centrifugal force as you rotate the glass to keep the olive circling the inside of the glass all the way to her hand.

Performance: Centrifugal force will get the olive from the table to her hand. This is due to the fact that a wine glass has tapered mouths that are smaller in circumference than the glass itself. Place the glass over the olive and start moving the olive around the inverted mouth while on the surface. The olive will start to rise up inside the glass as you keep spinning. Keeping the olive spinning in the glass, continue to rotate the olive while lifting upward to her hand. Stop rotating and let the olive fall out onto her hand.

Copy Cat

The Bet: Two shots are presented. You bet they cannot do as you do. You are clear that there are no actions the spectator is not capable of doing.

Secret: They swallow and you don't!

Performance: Make up a series of movements that are easy. Lift a glass. They do it. Move the glass. They do it. Move a napkin. They do it. Eventually, drink your shot. They do it. Pause, then spit your drink back out because you never swallowed! They can't because they certainly swallowed. You might consider taking one small sip, then talk a bit, then take another sip where you don't swallow to win the bet.

Head Through Card

The Bet: Bet that you can stick your head or foot through a business card.

Secret: The secret is an accordion cutting technique. The business card legitimately will stretch open enough for your head.

Performance: Borrow a business card. Bend it in half the long way. You will have two very short sides and two very long sides. With a pair of scissors, you are going to cut the business card like a comb with lots of eighth inch teeth. You need to cut into the fold of the card but be careful to not cut all the way to the other edge. Leave a good eighth of an inch or more all around your cuts. Once you have gone from one end of the card to the other, flip the card around. You will now cut in between all the cuts except the outermost cuts. So, from the side of the card that has the edges of the two halves, cut in between all the cuts you made from the other side. Here is the final phase of set up. Open the card and lay it flat. Without cutting the first and last tooth (the very edge on each end), slide a pair of scissors over the first strip and cut all the remaining

centers of the teeth you have created. Do not cut the last one. Once you are done, the card will accordion open and be surprisingly strong enough to hold together as you stretch it open for your head to go through.

Stood Up

The Bet: Bet that you can drop a match box onto its end and it will stay standing. They get several attempts first but fail.

Secret: The secret is to open the matchbox halfway before dropping it.

Performance: Get a matchbox and keep it closed. Drop it around the table from different heights and watch it land in different ways. Bet that you can drop it from a foot in the air and it will land on its edge first try. It is self working if you pull the drawer out half way before dropping the matchbox!

You said Black!

The Bet: You bet you can make them say the word "black." In no time at all, they loose when they say it.

Secret: They think you messed up and say the word by mistake.

Performance: Bet you can make them say "black". After they agree, get them to tell you the color of several items around the table. Ask the color of your eyes. Ask the color of the napkin. Ask the color of the table. Then quickly ask them the color of the american flag. When they say, "Red, white and blue." Immediately say, "HA! I told you I could make you say blue!" They are going to say exactly what you just thought, "You said black..." Now you made them say black!

Hard as Ice

The Bet: Bet that you can pick up an ice cube with a string out of a glass of water and they can't.

Secret: Salt will adhere the string or hair to the ice cube!

Performance: Take a string and tie a loop in the end like a lasso. Dip into a glass and try to get a piece of ice caught. When it looks impossible, let someone else try. Once they give up, take the bet. The secret is to lay the string onto the ice and then take the table salt and sprinkle it onto the string and ice! You can also do this with a piece of long hair from the girl! The salt causes the ice to stick to the string! If you put too much, you just might get all the ice to stick to the string as one big chunk.

Pick Up

The Bet: Bet that they cannot lift an empty bottle with a straw. They are not allowed to touch or invert the bottle.

Secret: The secret is to bend the straw about 1/3 of the way and push it into the neck.

Performance: Demonstrate trying to lift the bottle by doing it wrong. Try to grab, hook and tilt the bottle onto the straw following the rules. Let them try. Take the bet. This is when you bend your straw back on one end. Stick it in and pull it back. Once the straw pops partially open inside, it leverages it such that it allows you to lift the bottle! If the bend pops open all way way once pushed inside, you probably need to bend it longer. Play with this since each bottle has a unique shape.

Three Cups and a Girl

The Bet: You bet you can flip three glass to get them to end all face up and they cannot. Two glasses are turned at a time and in three flips they must all end face up.

Secret: When you successfully flip the glasses, you do not set it back up the same way for them to attempt it.

Performance: Start with three glasses lined up on the table. Arrange the glasses with the outer glasses face down and the

center glass mouth up. To successfully flip them all face up, start with the two on the right. Flip them. Next, flip the outermost glasses. Lastly, flip the right two again. Bet that they cannot do it in three moves like you did. After they take the bet, reset the glasses alternating again by flipping the center glass for them. However, if you remember when you started, it was not the center glass that was upside down! This discrepancy will fly right by. You both start with glasses alternating up

and down. However, you start with two down. They start with two up. They cannot get them all face up in only three moves!

Balanced Money

The Bet: You bet that you can balance a coin on the edge of a dollar.

Secret: After attempting and demonstrating, you bend the dollar to pull it off successfully.

Performance: Start off trying to holding a dollar on its edge. Try to hold a coin on the top edge and let go. Of course, the bill and coin will fall. Try this type of misleading set up before taking the bet. Once they see you trying this and they have tried it, they will take the bet. Bend the dollar in half and lay it on the table in a slight "V" with one edge down. Place the coin on the top centered over the "V".

Unopened Bottle Bet

The Bet: You bet you can drink from an unopened bottle.

Trick: It's a play on words.

Performance: Tell a a girl that you can drink from an un-opened wine bottle. (Or any bottle that has a concaved bottom that you can find). After the bet is made, take the bottle, turn it upside down and pour something into the recessed bottom of the bottle. Drink it and you have won the bet!

Got the Quarter

The Bet: A quarter is placed under a beer bottle and you bet you can get it without touching the bottle.

Secret: She lifts the bottle for you! Plus, you have a second coin to trick her.

Performance: This is a simple bar bet but gets a good laugh! Put a quarter under her beer and say that you can remove it without touching it. Have a second quarter hidden in one of your hands. Reach under the table and get the coin you are hiding to your finger tips. Act like you pull the coin through the table and show the coin. She will not believe you and remove the beer to check. When she does, grab the coin and say, "I told you I could get that quarter without touching the bottle!" This same trick can be done with a shot under a hat.

Pool Ball Bet

The Bet: Stick two balls together against a far rail. Another ball is balanced on top of the balls and the rail not touching the table. You bet you can take one shot with the cue ball and only hit the top ball. Of course, you win the bet!

Secret: You get the ball to drop between the other two by bumping the table!

Performance: In order to set this up, take two balls and hold them together against a rail. Using another ball, tap them on the top to keep them in place on the table. Place this third ball balanced on top of the other two resting on the rail itself. From the other end of the table place the cue ball and get a girl to take the bet. Say you can take one shot from where the cue ball is and hit the top ball without hitting the other two. After she takes the bet, smile and bump the table as you lightly take the shot. In fact, take a soft shot straight at the center of the two balls, then lightly bump the table. There is plenty of time if you take a slow shot. The two balls at the end will split and the third ball on top will fall down and roll towards the center of the table. It's a very easy shot! Just aim at the center of the two touching balls when you bump the table.

Scams

Phone Number

Tell her you can figure out her phone number without her telling you it. Act as if you are going to do a mind reading trick by asking her to write down her phone number on a piece of paper or napkin so you can't see. Say that you will predict the numbers and write them on another piece of paper. As you seem to concentrate, actually write *your* number little by little to make it seem believable. When you compare, she'll think you suck at mind reading. As you exchange papers, remind her that you *did* figure out her phone number without her telling you! Say it was more of a trick than mind reading, but it seemed to work just fine! Give her your number and best of luck!

Undercover Drink

Notice when your dream-girl gets a fancy drink. Walk up and cover her new drink with another glass inverted. Quickly tell her that, "I bet you a dollar that I can drink the contents of the bottom drink without touching the top glass whatsoever. After she accepts the bet, simply remove the glass and drink her drink. Give her a dollar and say, "Thanks, that was the cheapest $10 drink I've ever had!". Now, of course, you have broken the ice and can buy her a new drink!

Surprise!

Once you feel like you have a good thing going, ask a girl if she likes surprises. If she says yes, immediately kiss her. If she says no, kiss her anyways as say, "Oh, I forgot, you don't like surprises!"

Palms Up

Palm reading is not so much a scam as it is a tool to get closer and intimate. You would need to study a lot of cold reading and human tendencies to get good at this but it does not take much effort at all to use it for breaking the ice or hitting on a lady. Simply take a girl's hand and turn it face up as if you are going to do some palm reading. This position is recognizable enough that they will understand what you are attempting. Tell them that you can read things about their life, present and future. From this point on, you can wing it. That's right, wing it! You have probably just never tried this but you'd be amazed how fun and easy it is to fake your way through it. Tell them what you see about them. Tell them what they want to hear. If they seem sweet, tell them that. If they appear to care about their looks, tell them that. You could even be funny and tell them that you see a wonderful, clever man in their near future and then perfectly describe yourself! Have a couple predetermined lines made up and be aware that almost everyone is thinking about love, work, money and stresses of life.

Here's your Bill

In what looks to be a bet, you are actually loosing on purpose. Create a bet that you can easily loose. It can be anything. Bet her that you'll give her a hundred dollar bill if you can do whatever you decide. Loose the "bet" and proceed to give her a piece of paper that has printed across the top "This is a Bill". Within the page have lines for contact information which you will then ask for! There will be a line item for fun conversation and good times with a price of $100. So, you see, you told her that you would give her a hundred dollar *bill* and you have. You have charged her for your time and more to come. You should get a great laugh out of this and her information! You can tell her that you can waive your fees if you go out again to pay off her debt!

Mistaken Identity

Approach a girl from the side or back and grab them like you know them. Perhaps, hug them with excitement or even kiss them. Act as if you are connecting with one of your best friends in the world. Say, "I'm so glad you are here! How are you..." Then be completely shocked and embarrassed when you *discover* it isn't her! Say, "I'm so sorry to interrupt you... you look just like my friend who said she would be down here with friends. She's the most beautiful girl I've ever seen... the resemblance is amazing. I'm just so embarrassed... you both have even have the same taste in great clothes and have great figures..." The ice should be quite broken at this point to continue with any trick, come back later or see where it goes.

Picture Perfect

When standing or sitting next to your dream-girl, place your phone out so it can be be seen. If your phone has the option of flipping though pictures, do so. In fact, have a great screensaver always showing. Girls like cute pictures of dogs, friends, fun events and travels. Do not look too obvious, but you'd be surprised at how easy it is to have someone comment when they happen to glance at a fun photo.

Broken Phone

Another technique to using your phone as a tool is to act like you don't think your phone is working properly. After fiddling with it and "attempting" to make some calls, ask your dream-girl if she can call your number to hear if you can receive calls. Now you both have each others number.

That Feels Good

Act as if you are going to do some mysterious trick or prediction. Have them hold and rub your hand under the guise that something amazing is about to happen. As she holds your hand, have her look into your eyes and concentrate. Moments later, pause and exhale with pleasure and say, "Thanks, that has nothing to do with the trick, it just feels really good!" After a slap or laugh, continue with a real trick to break the ice some more. This is also a funny gag to do during a legitimate trick.

Tricks to Pick Up Chicks Book

Take this book with you the next time you approach a girl. Tell her that a friend gave it to you and you want her opinion about a couple lines or tricks. In doing so, you will engage her in conversation and break the ice!

Mystery Chain Call

If there is a pay-phone or establishment phone when you are out, get the number. When someone from a group of friends with your dream-girl are near, call the phone and ask for one of them by describing them. Say something like "I'm supposed to meet someone there... they should be wearing... tall guy with beard..." As you watch from a distance, just describe someone obvious. Once they are on the phone, the person will act confused. As soon as they are asking what you want, do the same thing to them and get the next person around on the phone. Person after person, see how long you can keep this up. Always mention they are with a really attractive girl you want them to introduce you too. About now, you'll want to make your way over to your dream-girl and say that you and friends are making bets and that she needs to take the call. It will all be confusing but funny to anyone with a personality. By the way, this is hilarious to do to perfect strangers on pay-phones on the street.

Blind Date

Once you spot your dream-girl at a party or bar, walk around like you are looking for a blind date that is supposed to meet you. After you notice she has seen you looking around, walk directly up and say, "Sarah? No? I was hoping you were her. My friend is having us meet here and he described her as..." Continue to essentially describe this dream-girl and add that this girl you are supposed to meet is supposed to be quite beautiful. Explain that you're sorry for interrupting but you were certain based on who else is at that place. You might even tease her and say, "You aren't just saying this because you aren't into me are you? You really aren't Sarah? I wish you were!"

Drunk

This is especially fun for people who do not drink much. Act as if you are pretty drunk with your friends. Proceed to laugh, be loud, stumble around and do whatever you want. You are drunk and you are one of two things in people minds. One, a total idiot to be avoided. Two, a guy having a good time who they will certainly put up with and laugh with. It's your job to make it go the fun route. It is easy if you keep your comments fun, strange, goofy and interesting. Stumble your way over to your dream-girl and hang all over her telling her that you'r going to marry her someday. Tell her that she is the most beautiful thing you've ever seen. Tell her whatever you want since you apparently have a free ticket to be a fool! Once she is taking care of you and listening to your drunken stories, make your move and/or instantly become sober. Depending on the setting and the type of girl you are going for, it should make sense how to adjust your behavior accordingly.

Earpiece

Wear your hands free earpiece for your phone if you have one. Get near your dream-girl and look towards her and say something like, "Hey there... I think you are so cute... I've had my eye on you for some time now..." and see her reaction to you. If it is positive, continue with anything nice like a drink offer or a trick. If the reaction is negative, keep talking and walking as if you weren't looking at her but just sort of gazing into space while on the phone with someone and look annoyed that she's trying to interrupt you! After the call ends, say, "Sorry, did you say something to me?" She will often feel embarrassed and be real receptive to some tricks if you play your cards right.

Fake Bet

An oldie but goodie is to simply approach a girl and tell her that your friends have bet that you would not approach the hottest girl in room. Ask if you can make them believe that you are making your move and just hang out showing her a few tricks. Act cool as if you could not really care. Have a great time doing some tricks and say thanks for helping out. You two will have a laugh about scamming your friends. All the while, you get exactly what you wanted. You got through the door and showed her you are cool. Now you have all the reason in the world to follow up.

Chapter 3 - "Threesomes"

Tricks, Scams & Set Ups
with your Wingman

Tricks with Your Wingman

With a friend's help, you gain a whole level of opportunities and fun. Be sure you and your wingman are familiar with your favorite tricks or scams in order to act fast on your toes. Some of these tricks rely on your friends ability to act uninvolved and be able to give you the credit. Just keep in mind that this is fun for all and not to legitimately take advantage of anyone. You should see how easy and flexible these tricks are depending on the setting, the attitude of the girls and your acting or B.S. skills. Again, I'll remind you to remember to be a gentleman even when scamming someone. Enjoy having "threesomes"!

Coin Prediction

Have nine coins laid on the table in a three by three grid. Turn away and have a girl point to any she wants. When you turn back around, you know which one she has picked! Your wing-man places his drink on the corresponding position on a napkin. Of course, this is done casually and you do not stare for your clue. It's quite easy enough to catch this tip with your peripheral vision. Secondly, this is your opportunity to hold the girls hand and ask her to concentrate while you try to figure out which coin she picked.

Bottle Caps

Place three bottle caps on a surface and ask for small coin like a penny or nickel. Turn around and ask your dream-girl to place the coin under one of the caps. You are going to guess where the coin is by using some sort of energy. If you prefer, you can ask her to kiss the coin to give it energy. Once it is hidden, turn back around and only stare at the bottle caps. If you had the girl kiss the coin, you could ask for a kiss on the cheek so you can feel for the energy of the coin. If you did not, just proceed to try to find the coin. When you are looking at the caps, place your hand over them and hover back and forth. When you have your hand over the correct one, your wingman signals you by taking a drink of his drink in the near background. Do not look around for a signal from them, just use your peripheral vision. Using energy to locate a hidden object like this looks very spooky and interesting. This will certainly make your dream-girl more curious about you.

Coin Toss

Play "Heads" or "Tails" with a girl. Your buddy does the flipping and you see who can get the most correct. Your buddy tells you the result by fingers completely touching together for heads and slightly opened for tails. Either he covers the coin on the table and signals with the hand that covers the coin or he watches your dream-girl do it and signals you with his hands. Of course, if you get your hands on a double headed coin, you can take this routine to another level by having your wingman use the double headed coin while you don't even look. As an additional signal, he can flip the coin while you are not looking and signal you by how he slams the coin onto the table. If he hits the coin down, it is heads. If he keeps the coin from hitting the table by pinching it with his thumb to deaden the noise, it is tails.

Word Code

A girl gets to pick from several objects lined up on the table. You turn around so you cannot see her point to one of the objects. Your wingman cleverly tells you which object by a predetermined code. I like to use "Okay, we're Ready" for the Right object, "Okay, Look" for the Left object. You can make up endless codes easily that suit you and the amount of objects you play with. When she has pointed to the object, your friend tells you to turn around by saying something very innocent like, "Turn around and Concentrate." This could be a code for the Center. You can use simple signaling sentences based on alphabetical order or the amount of words in the sentence to signal which item!

Mind Reading

Mind reading will make any girl smile. Have your wingman stand behind her while she writes a prediction on a slip of paper or napkin. Immediately, he secretly writes the same thing on the last page of a small notepad. As you are giving her instructions to fold her paper up and hide it in her pocket, there is plenty of time for him to walk away or slyly prepare the notebook. Just a moment later, you ask for the notebook. It will be an easy matter to see what she wrote as it is written in a secret, predetermined place in the notebook. Of course, he could write this on a napkin and add it to a stack of napkins as well. If there is a stack of napkins or there are napkins available, have a stack next to the girl. Have the wingman write on a napkin while she does and place his secretly face down onto the stack. When she puts her napkin away for safety (perhaps in her bra), you can have her hand you the stack of napkins. Now when you flip the napkin up to write the prediction, it will be already written! To enhance the experience, *draw* a picture of what she has written if she only wrote a word. It will appear as if you are really in her head. If your wingman already drew it perfectly, pretend to draw. Show it.

Card in Bottle

This is a killer stunt with the aid of your wingman! Hold a deck of cards up so she can see the faces and you cannot. Move the cards across in front of her eyes so she can see that they are all different. As you spread the cards, ask her to point to a card. Stop spreading the cards at that point and have her remember the card by moving the section of the cards forward. Bring the cards back together and continue to push the cards onto her card to bury it into the rest of the deck as they pass by. Meanwhile, your buddy has seen which card from behind her. He has not made his presence known and walks off to get the same card from a duplicate deck. At this point, there are a lot of options. The best being that he puts the card into a beer bottle and asks the waiter or bartender to had it to you when you are ready. Meanwhile, you pretend you are going to find her card. Try a couple attempts by naming cards out loud. Say that you'll just buy her a beer because you aren't figuring out the card. When she gets her beer, the card she's thinking of will be looking right at her through the glass of the bottle! When starting this effect out, you could say that you'll buy her a beer if you can't figure out her card. Additionally, if you do not drink or are in a situation where there is no drinking, the card can be placed anywhere that can be pointed out. I enjoy placing them inside of a menu or outside a window. If your wingman has some sort of skills, he can even ditch it in the pocket of her jacket, her purse or even under her butt from behind.

Impossible Aces

A deck of cards are shuffled and you never touch them. You will have a girl cut the cards anywhere she wants into four piles and deal cards as directed. The top of each pile is turned over to be all Aces! Do this by having the four aces already on top of the deck. Take out your cards and casually ask "some guy" to be part of this trick. Get your wingman to shuffle the cards while keeping the aces on top. He can easily split the cards and do a stand riffle shuffle but allow the aces to drop last. He can also learn the basic false *Overhand Shuffle* from the Magic Techniques section in Chapter 2. Once the cards are shuffled, have him hand them to the girl. Make a big deal about how you do not want to touch the cards. Have her cut most of the cards and move them to the right of the deck. Have her cut this section leaving about a third of the cards. Finally, have her cut the pile again in half and move it to the right. She should have cut and made four fairly equal piles. The last pile still has the aces on top. At this point instruct her to take the first pile on the left and pick it up (This will be the pile left first from the cutting.) Tell her to deal three cards on the table where the stack came from and one card onto each other pile. Then take the next pile and do the same. Again for the third pile. Up to this point, the only thing that has happened is the aces now have three random cards on top of them. Lastly, the fourth and final pile will be done. By putting the three cards where the last pile came from down into the table like before gets rid of the extra cards above the aces. When you place a card on each other pile, you are now placing the aces on each pile! It is all self working, just follow the instructions. You could do this trick on your own, but having your wingman shuffle the cards will make it look that much more impossible.

Telephone

Here's a great trick to get a number and read someone's mind. Let her shuffle the cards and take the deck back. When you take it back, casually notice what the bottom card is. Next, let her take any card she wants. Have her place it on top of the deck after she has remembered it. Be very certain that she takes it, remembers it but absolutely lets nobody around see it. Once her card is on top of the deck, give the deck a cut. Do not shuffle, only cut the cards. You may let her cut the cards as well. Here's the first phase which is pretty cool in itself. Turn the cards over and spread through them so you can see the faces. Look for the card you peeked at earlier. Her card is always the next card toward the bottom of the deck because when you cut, you place that card on top of hers! So, you know her card. You have lots of options to "read her mind" and tell her the card. Here's how to utilize your wingman. Looking at the cards, just name a couple out loud like you are struggling to figure out the card she picked. Tell her that you learned this from a magician and that maybe you need to call him and see if he can tell her. Call your friend who is already nearby and is waiting for this call. When he picks up, he will immediately start saying, "Hearts, Clubs Spades, Diamonds..." Interrupt him when he say the correct one by saying, "Hey magic man!" He will immediately start saying, "One, two, three, four, five..." You listen like he could be saying anything. It's completely normal looking to her. When he gets to the correct card value, say, "Hey, I'm calling to have you talk to a friend about a trick, hold on..." Immediately hand the phone over and he does the rest. It will be quite confusing when she explains the trick that is not working and he replies with the correct card because she picked one herself, showed nobody and knows you didn't signal anyone.

Scams with Your Wingman

Save Her

Your wingman approaches your dream-girl and is a total idiot. You see she is annoyed and needs saving. Walk up and interrupt them and show him that he is hitting on a taken girl. Say, "Hey babe, I'm sorry I'm late. Hey man, I think you hit on the wrong girl. Here's a couple bucks, go grab a beer and take it easy." He'll show great respect and gratitude to you both and walk away. Now here's your chance to say that it looked like she was being annoyed and you just wanted that guy to vanish. Tell her that she caught your eye and you couldn't just sit and do nothing while someone was obviously bugging her.

Redo

Don't you have those moments in life where you wish you could have said or done something different, especially in front of a girl? Why not reenact them with your wingman. Here's your chance to look cool, confident and in control. Perhaps, he wants to fight or argue about something near her and you take care of the situation. Use that perfect comeback you wish you could have done years ago. Use a type of hypnosis to calm him down or use a strange energy to get him to submit. Consider saying nothing and just give him a look. No need to be a cocky jerk here. Just handle it confidently without any risk of being played or hurting each other.

Blind Ambitions

Your buddy helps you to a seat next to a girl. You act blind. He places your drink and straw in your hands. Eventually, your wingman leaves you sitting next to your dream-girl and he asks if she can keep him company while he gets something.

Or your wingman says out loud to you, "You stay here for a second. You will be okay? Do you need anything right now?" to make it clear without telling her that you have a little vision problem. Once your wingman steps away, call for him. Look right toward her with a bit of a hundred yard stare into nothing and say his name again. She'll be sure to tell you that your friend is gone and will be right back. Strike up a conversation with her. Maybe tell her she has a great voice. Eventually ask to "see" her with your hands and feel around her body if you have the guts. It's up to you how long you want to keep this up. I know a guy who went for a long walk holding hands with this horrible scam!

Perfect Call Timing

After approaching a girl, have a wingman time a call to you. Take the call. This will do a few things. One, makes you look like you have friends and other things to do. Two, it gives you a chance to see her reaction to your call. To make her more curious, you could play it off like a girl is calling. Even better, you could tell the caller that you are busy with something important. After the call, you could take a picture of both of you to "send to your friend". What you are really up to is creating some intimacy, mystery and curiosity. Three, this gives you an excuse to run if she is just not worth the effort.

Issue Advice

Have a wingman text you with relationship problems. Turn to your dream-girl and ask her what you should do. This can be legitimate if the wingman is cool with it. Sitting close and talking about relationships is nice and intimate. However, avoid talking about your own relationships.

Hit On Set Ups

Prank to Prank

Have your wingman go up to the girl you are interested and tell her that he wants to pull a prank on you. He tells her that you think she's the hottest girl here and he wants to mess with you. Your wingman asks if she will pretend to be interested in you! She accepts and she thinks that your wingman returns to you telling you that she wants you to come over. Of course, you will have fun talking to her because the scam is really on her. The door is open and you have nothing to loose. Later, if your wingman comes over and laughs with her that she was messing around, it really doesn't matter because the ice has been broken and you will know if she is worth continuing to have fun with.

Pool Sharks

When playing pool or even a drinking game, board game or whatever, have your wingman grab a small group of girls to join in. So you look clean, he conveniently pairs up teams with you and your dream-girl!

Built Up

Stand near your dream-girl. Create a solid impression by having your wingman come over and talk to you like you are the best thing since sliced bread. Have him talk about how fun and amazing you were at the last event you guys went too. If the chance arises, have your wingman lean over to the girl and say, "Have you seen the tricks this guy can do?" Have him create enough hype and interest in you that she will be curious about what you can do. Act as if it is no big deal and show her and your wingman a cool trick. It can easily be one of the tricks in the book that your wingman is in on.

Coincidence

Have your wingman approach the girls you want to talk to you. Before they are given enough time to decide if they like him or not, you come over and catch up on old times with him as if you just ran into each other. Eventually, you can ask who his friends are if that has not worked itself out already. Girls like to see good communication, fun, laughter and wit between guys. If you make each other look cool, they will like the show. Be sure to have them hear how you are not afraid of anything. Girls like to know that you can take care of yourself and them if need be. Keep in mind that you are just trying to break the ice here. Try not to become a secret agent and build a friendship on lies. You might consider laughing at the girls later once you are all hitting it off by explaining they fell for the oldest trick in the book. This will depend on your style and motives.

Play in the Gap

A way to take advantage of traffic at a bar is to sit with your buddy at a bar far apart. Bars get busy and groups of girls will have no choice but to find a gap to order their drinks. Having a wingman that sits further than normal might be a great way to cast a net together. Lines can get long and you will find your-self almost having no choice but to talk to someone in line since they are cutting of your conversation with the wingman.

Scavenger Hunt

Both of you run up to your dream-girl with a list of things you have to make happen for a scavenger hunt contest. The other has to be a witness. You get to her first and he "honors" it and lets you go. You say you had to find the cutest girl and get her to complete the following tasks. He then reads from his list things you have to do with her. You can create your own based on the setting, your personalities, etc. Good starters are guessing things about her and you have to keep guessing until you get ten correct. Obviously, you'd want to lead up to getting a kiss, a date or a phone number. It's a good way to get away with nearly anything to break the ice. You guys could run off afterwards or just end up with her by ending the game by saying, "Aw, Man... You won. You actually got to a hundred points before me." The possibilities are endless with this excuse to barge in on someone.

Chapter 4 - Body Language

Learn What She's Really Thinking!

Body language is a huge key to knowing when you have a green light to come play! I'll share what I call "shifts" in movement. Watch for how your dream-girl shifts or adjusts her breathing, movement, seating, looking and more while sitting or interacting. Keep in mind, these give you an advantage but they do not make you a mind reader. For instance, if someone is in a horrible mood but are attracted to you, they very well may still portray a closed off body language. Knowing how to read them will give you a head start since you'll have the correct frame of mind when you approach them. Also, knowing how to read others around her can make life easier.

Keep in mind that subconscious or natural signs are accurate. On the contrary, if someone is trying to portray an attitude or is acting, you can bet they are insecure, playing a game and more nervous than you. Knowing ahead of time what you are dealing with gives you a great advantage. Use these tips to decipher the language of the body of your dream-girl!

1. If you make eye contact with your dream-girl, keep a subtle eye on her immediately afterwards to see if she plays with her hair, licks her lips, nibbles her lip, looks for you or fiddles with something in her hands. If she does alter her state and reveals these tells, she is likely into you and will accept your approach.

2. A similar look to when a girl is caught looking at you after your first glance is this deeper desired look. This is found if there have been multiple exchanges and she is caught deeply entranced. Notice how the look conveys that she hears or sees nothing else. See how her head is aimed at her prize?

3. If her body position adjusts toward you and she leans toward you, make your move. Remember, some of the easiest things to spot are shifts. If she shifts away, she is retreating. If she shifts toward you, she is interested. It is quite easy once you get it and see it.

4. If a body opens up to you including legs or feet opening apart, that is a strong sign of attraction. However, be aware if there are other players in the area that might be causing her to be comfortable or interested. In this case, she is very interested. See the hands face up and relaxed? Notice the legs not touching for comfort.

5. Many signs are subconscious to the lady. For instance, if she turns toward you or opens her hands upwards exposing her palms or wrists, she is signaling for you to make your move.

6. When a woman adjusts her skirt and legs in slow motion, it may be a sign she's attracted. Think about it, when you are not caring about someone near you, you just do things easily and naturally. When a girl crosses her legs slowly, it means she's trying to get your attention or is distracted by you in some way.

7. If a woman lets her shoe come off her heal and lets it dangle by her toes while looking at you, she is likely interested.

8. When feet shift, you can learn a lot. When feet shift forward, it usually means comfort or confidence. However, when feet shift back, under or curl around a chair leg, it means retreat, lack of confidence or fear.

9. When you first shake hands with your dream-girl, notice her hand position. If she met you half way, there is balance. If her hand was palm up, she is giving you control. If she turns your hand face up and hers face down, she is taking charge. This goes for men or women. If her hand extends far out with a locked elbow, she has not warmed up to you yet. If you evaluate handshakes, what you see is what you get. Strong, controlling, weak, confident, suspicious, careful, scared, insincere and much more can easily be read.

Notice the woman is clearly on top. Men are not often submissive, so this is a sign of a woman clearly taking charge and displaying high confidence.

Notice the man either being in control and/or the woman being submissive.

10. When a girl enters your personal space to whisper in your ear, even when it might be a bit loud, she is encountering in a one of many intimate signals. Remember, unless she leans in to say, "Get lost", she's comfortable being close to you.

11. Change in dilation of the eyes is an interesting sign of attraction. In fact, many photographs are altered in ads to have large black pupils as it makes the person feel more attractive! You are concerned with the *change* of dilation. Try to notice if they get bigger when you look at her. If they change to larger, she very well may be attracted to you or what you are doing. Obviously, in dark rooms, the eyes will naturally be dilated bigger and in bright light, they will appear smaller. It is the change from any condition you are looking for.

12. If she smiles big when you make eye contact, you are solid. Go talk! A *genuine* smile is gold.

13. If she laughs at your comments, gestures or tricks, she enjoys being around you.

14. If you make eye contact and you keep seeing that she's looking at you, take another look back and smile. If you catch her again, she is interested enough to see some entertainment. If she plays with her hair and looks toward you, she is very interested.

15. If a girl doesn't open up to you and looks around, you do not have her attention. Either do or say something interesting or cut your losses. If she can't keep her attention on you, why waste your time? Of course, we all look around so don't just cut her off when she is normal. This shows a disconnect and uninterested lady who has better things to do... like be alone.

16. People have a built in mimic or matching trait. We often copy the things we like. If you really want to play mind games, take a drink or check your phone. Wait a few seconds and notice if she does the same. If she was aware of you, she could copy your lead. Now you know she's checking you out.

17. Beware if a woman rolls her eye in your presence. She could be signaling to you and her friends that she is not interested. You don't want a group of friends making it hard for you. Either turn your attention to someone else, call her out, do something amazing or leave her hanging as *you* leave.

18. If a persons arms are crossed, they are closed off. It's probably better to spend some time entertaining someone else. However, assess the situation and make sure she is just not uncomfortable and might use some entertainment! There is a difference between uninterested and insecure. Did you *cause* her arms to cross or was she already closed off?

19. FBI profiling digs into the meaning of legs and feet more than most fields looking at body language. If legs cross when you are near, she is likely not interested and is closing off. However, if she is pointing towards you and they are crossed, she may be interested but is nervous about something.

20. If a girl is sitting with legs crossed and the front leg moves in a back and forth kicking motion, she is likely bored. Go give her some fun interaction. Be sure to observe that she looks bored and not impatient as she would if she was waiting for someone that is late.

21. When you see a shift in feet, you will gather very honest and accurate information. Girls are often very aware of their eyes and upper body, but never think about the position of their feet. If you see her feet shift to a pigeon toed type look with her feet touching, she may be uncomfortable or insecure. Legs out front and comfortable means she's at ease.

22. If anyone leans away from you, chill the heck out! There is no reason to be pushy or get to a point to where you are getting such a strong "get away" signal. You do not want to ever get this message as others will label you as well.

23. When a girl peeks back over her shoulder and exposes her neck with a gentle glance back to you, it is flirty and inviting. Especially if her head is not turned all the way, but her eyes follow you, go say, "Hello."

24. Micro-expressions take a bit of training to decipher. In general, they are facial expressions that happen the instant the person has a reaction. Even if they are trying to hide it, a subconscious flash of a reaction can occur. From frowns, smiles, shock, guilt and more, this snap shot is quite accurate of their true feelings. In this picture, one fraction of a second before or after and you'd never know she was stressed in any way by whatever the guy just said. I know it was *what he said* and not *what he did* because she is looking him in the eyes. There is not enough time to be watching his hands or trick, make this micro-expression and look back at his eyes. It happened this very instant.

25. You can tell the difference between a nose, eye or neck scratch gesture vs. a legitimate itch. If they make this as a gesture, they are often not in agreement with what you are doing or saying, or if they do not know what to do. If they do not know they are doing it, it is subconscious. Remember, you know what a real itch looks like. A real itch is fast and direct.

26. Clenched hands and rubbing hands are a sign of concern. Subconsciously, if you do a trick that requires her to use her hands and stop clenching, she will open up much more. Breaking a pacifying behavior can change a person's mood entirely.

27. If you see a shift of hands to the neck dimple area, be careful that you are not making her nervous or uncomfortable. Some people do not like being tricked or put on the spot. You want to break the ice, not disturb your lady. When a girl covers her neck or holds her hand flat to her chest, she is concerned, stressed or fearful.

28. Body contact can be confusing in crowded places. Keep an eye out for the "accidental" brush by. If you feel a girl brush by you, do anything but ignore it. Pretend to be offended. Talk to her. Follow her. Do anything but think it is normal, especially if she smiles at you.

29. Hair stroking can be confusing. If a girl is alert, licking her lips and playing with her hair, she may be aroused. If she is pulling, holding, or stroking her hair with a blank look in her eyes, she may be doing it to pacify herself and may be very well upset at the situation. In this case, it appears as if the girl is uncomfortable with something she sees. This is not something that means leave her alone. In fact, she might need a little pick me up! You aren't the one that made her feel this way.

Here, the example is taken to more of an extreme to show a complete disconnect. This girl is likely sad about something.

30. If you see your dream-girl with her fingers all touching like a steeple, it is a strong sign of confidence, but sometimes smug or egotistical. Regardless, you aren't playing with a pushover. Bring your "A" game.

31. A combination of reactions due to attraction by a woman may include moving her legs toward you, head-cocking, exposure of the thighs, protruding breasts, and slowly stoking wrist or thigh.

32. A sign of acceptance or readiness is shown by a woman when she leans forward in her chair, legs uncross and hands on knees. This is a similar look to someone that is excited and about to get up.

33. If a girl reaches out to grab your arm or smack you during any of your set ups or tricks, she playfully getting closer to you. This is a very good sign.

34. When someone rubs their legs or knees with their palms, they are subconsciously trying to comfort themselves.

35. Always show respect and understand that "No means no." That said, there is a truth to "No means yes." Let me explain. If there is an honest sign that is immediate that reveals "No", then it is accurate. However, strange enough as it may sound, when it is highly acted or forced, it may mean that she is truly interested but has another layer to the game you have to decipher. Often, just the next drink, joke, trick, smile, laugh or smart ass remark may make her open up. In fact, in a poker game, top psychologists will say that the person with the best hand may sigh as if they are really pulling their nails out to make the call - when in fact, they have the best hand and are covering their excitement.

36. If someone's body position and legs are pointing towards an exit instead of people or action, they might wish they weren't there. Often, you'll see head in hands and a disconnected look as well.

37. Eyes squinting in the midst of some interaction may show distance and high discomfort. Of course, this is a shift you are looking for. Merely squinting could mean a draft, dry eyes, bad vision and more. However, if they have a sudden look of being taken back and squint due to you, you better make amends real fast. Don't confuse this with a slow, *dreamy* closed eye effect caused by arousal.

38. Be very careful of eye closing, rubbing and blocking. If she attempts to block her eyes from seeing you or your game, she is telling you she's not interested in something. You might bust out your quickest trick or joke to bring her back to earth.

39. Try to be confident enough to return any gestures of touch. Without getting into it deeply, at the DNA level it will cause her to respond well if you return any touches she throws your way. However, be certain that your touches are equal. There is a dance happening below the surface you should be aware of. If she gives you a little bump, grabs your shirt, lightly slaps you on the arm or anything playful, be sure to give some sort of affection back in return.

40. A high sign of stress is seen with the mouth. If she covers her mouth with her hand, puts her finger across her lips or bites her tight lips, she is likely concerned or even guilty with something going on in that moment. Be careful that she isn't just shy due to bad teeth. Also, don't confuse playing with lips and liking lips as that is a high sign of arousal. Lastly, I'll note that some people with high intelligence often hold themselves like this naturally. Look for a shift *to* this behavior, not a natural occurrence of this look.

41. A gesture of interest and suggestion to come over is shown when a lady's position is toward you. The head may be turned a little or tilted, but the body is directed towards you and her arms are sometimes stretched out onto the knees in almost a cute or flirty manner. This can be highly enhanced by stroking the hair and slow down-casting eyes.

42. Keep in mind that there is a big difference between a girl comforting herself because you are making her nervous and when she is uncomfortable all on her own. People are often uncomfortable in settings. If you see a girl being slightly un-comfortable without a reaction to something, be cool and go charm her. I'll bet she is just a little bored and uncertain what to do. Her's your chance to put a smile on her face.

43. Clearly, the girl pictured below has had enough. She is comforting herself by rubbing her neck, but is also showing a sign of irritation by looking away and compressing her mouth. You may have made her upset with your comments or pushiness. Remember, there is a big difference in the look of a girl comforting herself because she's uncomfortable on her own and when she is getting uncomfortable due to someone else.

44. If another guy that might be interested in the same girl looks at you and repositions himself directly towards you or your dream-girl, he very well may be taking a protective and aggressive position. Be careful if he makes his jaw stick out more and raises his head. That is a strong subconscious sign that he is trying to be dominant.

45. If another guy is rubbing his head, ears, forehead, neck or adjusts his shirt or crosses his arms, he might be getting upset that you are ruining his plans but is not aggressive enough to make a scene about it. In general, it's not good to make anyone squirm unless done blatantly out of cleverness or wit. It's better to use the guy in a trick or give him the upper hand on the girl as well so he does not ruin your game. If more people see you as fun, attractive or in charge, you will be much more attractive to your dream-girl.

Here's a good time to remind you that the signals of body language go both ways. What signal are you conveying? Be sure to be confident and let your body language work its magic. Without looking like you are on the prowl and sounding cheesy, you can convey that you want to get closer by comfortably taking advantage of many of the tells I've given. For instance, when sitting down next to a girl, what message would you be subconsciously telling her if your body was pointing away from her? The answer is obvious! You are telling her you want to leave-even if you don't! Now why would she want to spend time with someone already checking out? She wouldn't. The point is to remember that you might get familiar with reading people but don't forget that others naturally get a "feeling" themselves with no training at all. You are a big step ahead if you have a bit of a game plan and awareness. Good luck!

Chapter 5 - Rules of the Game

Tricks to Get Chicks!

Chapter 5 - Rules of the Game

Tips, Rules, Do's & Don'ts to Dating

1. When using a wingman, it might be even better to use a wing-woman. As an advantage to get your foot in the door, remember that it is sometimes easier for women to talk without their guard up compared to two guys approaching them. Also, girls are competitive when it comes to getting a man's attention. When they see you with a woman, they are much more likely to find you worthy of their time.

2. Women will be much more attracted to you if the people you are hanging out with are smiling at you or admiring you. Therefore, it's okay to just have fun around her with anyone. Impress the circle then you impress her.

3. Tricks alone won't necessarily impress girls. Find a way to convey your personality while you perform tricks.

4. Besides the ideas in this book, don't forget the rest of the common sense rules in life. You know, being a gentleman in addition to being cool, confident and fun. It does not make you less funny or cool to open doors, give a helping hand and being kind when the opportunity arises.

5. Go by how a girl *acts* and not by what she *says* if you are confused by her.

6. If you get a girl's number, consider sending her a text message by "mistake." Send a message to her on purpose that clearly looks extended for another girl. Try something like this, "I loved our walk at the park and laughing with you at the movies." Text something you obviously did not do with the girl you are sending this too. You have to decide on how great of a connection you had. If you are both love at first sight, this should be potentially avoided. However, in the causal dating world of first dates, this can make her really curious, jealous, competitive and eager to connect soon. If she calls you out about the mistaken message, obviously it was "meant" for someone else. "The names are in the phone right after each other."

7. If doing a card trick that requires a name to be signed on the card, always follow with "...and your phone number right there." Do this the instant they are finishing writing their name on the card and say it in a half joking tone. You'd be surprised how often they just do it for fun. If you are serious or not, this catches people off guard. Remember, most card tricks where a card can be chosen can have a name written on them for "verification" purposes later.

8. Don't ask obvious questions like, "How old are you?", "What do you do?", etc. Instead, be a little witty and ask, "You must make money somehow, do you like your job? I love hearing how people make a living..." Ask off beat questions like, "What's the coolest place you've ever been." Try to find ways to make tangental questions to show you are fun and creative. For instance, if she says she works with kids, immediately say something like, "Oh, what the heck do you do about all those germs! Don't you watch the news!?" If she says she likes water sports, say, "Are you crazy? Haven't you seen Jaws?"

9. Mystery breeds curiosity. Don't let on how your tricks work. Keep the mystery a mystery.

10. Try to get a girl to be interested, not just impressed. The goal of tricks is to gain her attention, not just trick her. If you can gain her interest, you are all set to her wanting more. In others words, don't try to pursue women, but rather make them attracted to you. Too many guys prowl and pursue.

11. Bragging and showboating are pointless and short term. Ambition, on the other hand will get attention.

12. When asking a girl to go out, dance, walk or whatever, show that you are interested but be sure to convey that you do not need her to have a good time. Have a frame of mind that you are not desperate and that you are going to have a great time with or without her... and that you'd really like her to be part of it. Be polite, confident and genuine but not needy!

13. Don't waste time chasing women that are not interested in you or interesting to you!

14. If a women tells you she has a boyfriend right away, respectfully say, "I'm sorry, I didn't know having a boyfriend kept people from making new friends. It was good to meet you anyways." Walk away and do not look back. If she lied, she may very well change her mind later. If a guy finally shows up, then it is better that you didn't interfere.

15. If you are in the position of arranging a call or meeting up again, do not leave it vague! Do not say, "Well, call me whenever and we'll get together sometime..." Be very clear that you will call her by the end of the week. Do not leave it unclear.

16. It's all about enjoying life. Entertain yourself with her and know that you will not win them all. It's not a big deal.

17. You can be very confident but try not to be too serious.

18. Do not ask permission. Just do the dang trick, make the move, give her a hug or ask her to join you. When asking for a number, don't say, "Can I get your number?" Instead say, "What's your number?"

19. Have a good handshake. In fact, a firm, controlled hand shake followed by a gentle covering with the left hand feels sincere and confident. Depending on the situation, you might test for personality here and go for the complex multi-handshake done between guy friends. This will throw her off and test if she has any personality at all. I'd save this tactic for casual meetings and not when you really want to impress someone.

20. Role reversal is fun. Act as if she is hitting on you!

21. Unless it is obvious love at first sight for both of you, leave them wanting more. Do not blow you wad, so to speak on all your tricks or conversation. It might be best to cut it all short so there is no awkward downtime. It's a good time to ask to see her again before you run out of ammo.

22. Be careful to not become a therapist or girlfriend. You can be genuine, caring and supportive but do not look or act like a pushover to her. Sometimes you can just change the subject and say you are not interested in gossiping or hearing about issues. Say your are a positive person and just want to have a good time with her because she seems like a cool chick.

23. Don't try to make her like you. Just be yourself and let the chips fall where they fall. If you are having a good time, she will. If not, she is not worth your time!

24. Worried that she might have given you a fake number? Just repeat it back with a couple numbers reversed to verify the number. If she corrects you, then the number is real. If she doesn't, then she probably doesn't know the number she gave you. Better luck next time.

25. Paying a compliment is sometimes hard for a guy because if we see something unique or interesting about a girl, we are not programed to comment on it like girls are. However, girls like it when you notice something unique about them or something they are wearing. Pick something more unique than the fact that they are hot. Be specific. Perhaps you might comment on their eyelashes, lips, skin, shirt, belt, shoes, bag or smile.

26. Playing with each other's personal belongings can create intimacy. For instance, let her play a game on your phone or look at some pictures. Grab her phone and ask what apps she has.

27. Practice tricks by yourself, then on your friends before ever trying them on a perfect stranger! Remain mysterious and fun with your tricks. Never reveal how anything is done or your will cheapen the experience and loose the mystery they have developed in you.

28. Hit and run. Tell a fast one-liner as you walk by and keep an eye on your dream-girl for the chance to come back later.

29. Be sure to make eye contact while performing your tricks.

30. Don't stutter or stumble. Make sure to practice your magic tricks rigorously so that you can be confident in your performance.

31. Jealous guys or girls might try to sabotage your pick-ups by heckling during your performance or revealing your magic secrets. Having solid magic skills can deflect these problems.

32. Never look intimidated by a beautiful woman! Beautiful women are used to men being intimidated by them and only find the men who aren't intimidated to be attractive.

33. Never talk negatively about yourself, your job your ex or anything! Remember, woman are searching for their companion too, so why would she want to share her time with someone that is not happy with themselves.

34. While talking to your dream-girl, constantly repeat her name. This will be like music to her ears. For example "Stop trying to hit on me, Jill... I know what you're up to!" instead of "Stop trying to hit on me... I know what you're up to!" Adding her name when possible creates a strong connection.

35. If you start to think someone is too good for you, just remember they also wipe their butts, get hungry, watch tv and wake up with bad breathe.

36. When talking, be sure to show ambition. Woman are attracted to go getters and aren't attracted to lazy and unmotivated men. You should strive to let everyone know that you are going places!

37. Never look at the ground while talking to your dream-girl. This is a sign of insecurity. Always have a positive, confident posture.

38. To some degree, we all have lots in common, but it is exciting when talking to let it reveal itself. Let her bring up some topics and if you have it in common tell her, "Me too!" or "I totally know what you mean, I..." Don't over use this as you want some mystery left! Unless you just dig this girl as a friend, show there are some great common interests, but leave something for later.

39. When exchanging numbers, let her put her number in your cell phone. It is intimate and allows you to immediately call her as you walk away! It is a fun and charming thing to do, but more importantly, it gives her your number. The idea of waiting a couple days to call her may still apply afterwards, but it is a very memorable moment to call within a minute!

40. Don't try to impress your dream-girl by telling her about things you've bought or own. Bragging is a big turnoff. There is a fine line between showing your are the man and bragging. Actions speak louder than words. Showboating, being in control or center of attention can be okay, but bragging is a huge killer.

41. Don't make it your goal to impress her with your tricks. Rather, make it your goal that you are both having a good time.

42. Remember the power of a simple joke. Every time she tells the joke, she will think of you!

43. It's quite okay if your "wingman" is a "wing-woman". In fact, in many cases, a girl will be more likely to look at you like you have something to offer if you are able to be friends with another girl... or look as if you are already taken. She might be happily surprised to find out you are available.

44. Never talk about an ex. If it comes up, try your best to stay positive. Say something like, "Oh, she was a wonderful girl, we just didn't see eye to eye. Sometimes things just don't work out." Then change the subject to something fun and interactive.

45. You will look like a fool if you ignore the friends of your dream-girl. In fact, there are many studies that show that your chances of success improve if you flirt more with her friends than her! We are not going to get into that type of game playing, but just remember to be cool to everyone. Show some respect and give some love to her friends in order to be looked at like someone she and her friends want around.

46. Do you prefer girls that are smiling? It goes both ways. Don't be a stick in the mud. Smile and show that you are enjoying talking to her. As simple as it is, smiling is one of the most powerful seduction weapons. It's easy, free and makes everyone more comfortable.

47. Be sure to be cool and smile at everyone around. You want everyone drawn to your magnetism. If you just focus your kindness toward your dream-girl, she wont pick up that everyone else likes you. When you are out with friends, look for those guys who are total punks to everyone. They do not get girls or friends. Girls do like confident, take charge, charismatic guys, but not social rejects.

48. Confidence is usually thought of as most important, but happiness is the best kept secret. If you convey that you are happy, you will win the hearts of many.

49. Don't ask if you can have a phone number, tell her to give it to you. This is done smoothly. For instance, do not be weak and ask, "May I have you number so I might call you sometime?" Instead, reframe it to simply leave it much harder to say no by saying, "I'd love to call you sometime, what is the best number to reach you?" It's simple psychology used by good waitresses. If you where asked "Do you want desert?" vs. "Which desert would you like to end the dinner with?... Our cake, pie or ice-cream?" The second does not really ask if you want desert, but rather which one. It's much harder to say no to that structure.

50. If rejected, remember it's a good thing! You didn't waste your time. Remember to be nice, smile and simply walk away.

51. Of course it does feel good if you are seen having a good time with others after being dismissed, but it really does not matter. Just let it go and keep a positive attitude. She is the one loosing out on someone with great personality. She'd rather be stuck with a complaining, lame guy. Just go and be happy she saved you your trouble.

52. It makes you all feel good when giving a compliment. Try it out. Do it to women anytime even if you are not interested.

53. If you are rejected, do not jump to the next closest girl to try your trick! You will look pushy and desperate. Stay cool and take your time meeting someone worth your time. Also, if you can tell she is looking around while you are talking or doing a trick, she is not worth your time. Rejection is coming so reject her first. Strangely, you often cause the girl to actually gain a newfound interest in you. As always, do not forget to be yourself and a gentleman. This is where guys hear about techniques and think being an ass is the right thing to do. It isn't.

54. Do not run up to a girl when she first enters a party, pool hall, bar or whatever. Give her a moment to adjust to the room a bit, kick her feet up, find her friends! I know that when you have a trick all planned, you are dying to spring it on someone, but be cool.

55. If a girl is really burning your hands with her eyes and you are nervous pulling off a trick, say, "Now I know how girls feel... You know, *my eyes are up here*! I feel so objectified!"

56. Just like the curiosity magic creates, leaving an incomplete message when you call them for the first time will too. If you are nervous about calling and potentially leaving a message and not having her call back, this will nearly ensure she'll call! What you do is leave a message with the first half of a important message. It could be something like, "Oh, I'm so bummed this went to voicemail. I have something very interesting to tell you. After we met, I was." Literally hang up mid talk. Two things happen. One, she calls back! Two, she picks up. Either way, you sarcastically say something like, "I knew I could make you call me!"

57. Leave them wanting more. Always. Also, be sincere but don't make it obvious you completely dig her. If she doesn't know if you like her or not, she will be psychologically unable to reject you and want to know more about you.

58. I shouldn't have to say it, but hitting on a girl while you have dirty nails, bad breath, stinky flip flops and wrinkled clothes is not going to get you far. Take care of yourself, wear nice shoes and look to kill. I'm not saying you have to be vain, but just be aware of the details. Woman will notice if you take care of yourself. Would you want to be with a girl with stinky feet and bad hair? I didn't think so. The whole "I don't care how I look" phase is over. There is a big difference between edgy and trashy.

59. When it comes to your wingman, know your roles and who's to ultimately benefit during a trick, scam or setup. However, don't forget to share the limelight with your wingman when the time comes. Even though you might use a *wing*man, it does not mean you wing it. In other words, make sure there's a good vibe between you and eliminate competition before you do a trick together. When you are secretly helping someone out, they must be able to receive all the credit and visa versa.

60. Have swagger or attitude if you want, but be yourself!

ACKNOWLEDGEMENTS

In an effort to support other creative entertainers around the world, I'd like to take a moment to give mention to those who have helped revive some of the bets and tricks that have been around for ages. Although the tricks in this book are partially credited to others, to myself or are open domain, the following magicians have made wonderful improvements, variations and new creations. I'd be remiss to leave out the names of those who are known for advancing or making popular many of the basic effects you have learned in this book.

Mac King for *poking* fun of magic with *"Something in my Eye"*

Daniel Garcia for *levitating* the art of butterfly origami

Michael Mode for new *twists* on the napkin rose

Dan Harlan for *stretching* the possibilities with rubber bands

Max Maven for *thinking* to do *"Elephant in Denmark" on TV*

Uri Geller for *bending* reality with spoons and forks

Gregory Wilson for *tying* up my time with *"ring on string"* tricks

I've been fortunate in my magic career with numerous original creations and top selling products. However, I know first hand how difficult it is to know where some very simple ideas or scams originated from. These are just a few of the leaders in the art of magic who have certainly shared a lot with us all.

Other products available from Rich Ferguson can be found at his official store at www.TheIceBreaker.com/store